Praise for

Integrative Attachment Family Therapy

"Dafna Lender's framework, integrative attachment family therapy (IAFT), uses the power of neuroplasticity to provide parents and children with new experiences of safety and connection that shift trauma-informed relationships. It offers a powerful mental health intervention that can help families to heal. If parents and therapists follow Dafna's guidance, they can make significant progress in reducing attachment trauma in future generations."

—**Bessel van der Kolk, MD,** #1 *New York Times* best-selling author of *The Body Keeps the Score*

"*Integrative Attachment Family Therapy* is a child-focused, multidimensional framework on the vanguard of treatments that heal and strengthen attachment issues in the parent-child relationship. With clear, accessible language and illustrative case examples, Dafna Lender shows how activities based in somatic practices can intervene in problem behaviors in children and in parents. The result is a comprehensive book that will benefit all mental health care professionals who strive to alleviate children's pain and reconstruct family functioning."

—**Peter A. Levine, PhD,** best-selling author of *Waking the Tiger: Healing Trauma* and *Trauma Through a Child's Eyes: Awakening the Ordinary Miracle of Healing*

"Dafna Lender presents an integrated therapeutic approach, IAFT, as an accessible, intuitive, optimistic, and compassionate strategy to strengthen the parent-child relationship. The product of this integration is a transformative therapeutic strategy that leverages the importance of both child and parent feeling safe enough to trust each other. Through clinical examples, we observe how this new felt sense of safety enables both the parent and child to become more accurate and respectful witnesses, a process that evolves into the parent-child co-regulation becoming more symmetrical and imbued with the resilience necessary to process potentially disruptive challenges that may confront either the child or the parent."

—**Stephen Porges, PhD,** author of *The Polyvagal Theory* and *Clinical Applications of the Polyvagal Theory*

"This book should be required reading for anyone who works with children. As experienced therapists know, no one clinical model is comprehensive enough to work for everyone. However, Dafna Lender's integrative attachment family therapy comes darn close. I am hard pressed to think of parents and children who would not be helped by her elegant approach. Through her gift of storytelling, complex ideas come alive in ways that are both poetic and practical. I can't recommend this illuminating book highly enough!"

—**Karen Doyle Buckwalter,** LCSW, RPT-S, author and podcaster

A Clinical Guide to Heal and Strengthen the Parent-Child
Relationship through Play, Co-regulation, and Meaning-Making

Integrative
Attachment
Family Therapy

Dafna Lender, LCSW, with Molly Gage
Foreword by Bessel van der Kolk, MD

INTEGRATIVE ATTACHMENT FAMILY THERAPY

Published by
PESI Publishing, Inc.
3839 White Ave
Eau Claire, WI 54703

Cover and interior design by Emily Dyer
Editing by Molly Gage

ISBN 9781683736844 (print)
ISBN 9781683736851 (ePUB)
ISBN 9781683736868 (ePDF)

PESI Publishing
pesipublishing.com

Table of Contents

Foreword

Over the past few decades our society has come to realize the profound effects that trauma, particularly early life trauma within one's caregiving system, has on the developing mind and brain. Trauma affects not only the person exposed to it but that person's family, friends, and larger community.

We carry trauma's imprints in our minds and hearts, and also in our biology and immune systems. Our brains and identities are shaped by our earliest realities, and exposure to violence, neglect, or other forms of trauma shapes our perception of danger, safety, and control. The legacy of trauma is most of all expressed in difficulties regulating one's emotional reactions and engaging in intimate reciprocal relationships—small obstacles may evoke catastrophic reactions or precipitate a complete shutdown.

Regardless of all the adversities we may experience, our minds, brains, and bodies are not immutably shaped by those events. We are adaptive, relational creatures whose minds and brains have ongoing capacities to change and adjust. Even if we have been profoundly impacted by trauma, we can harness our adaptive capacities to change our responses and relationships.

This understanding is critical when working with traumatized children and their families. These children's behaviors, the result of a pervasive sense of danger and vulnerability, are often marked by problems with impulse control, attention, and concentration. Naive teachers and mental health professionals often categorize these children as oppositional or defiant, as if they deliberately choose to create problems for themselves and those around them, when, in fact, they are simply reacting to a perceived danger from which they can see no escape.

The hallmark of traumatized children is having trouble feeling safe and forming trusting relationships. Their lack of secure attachment to their caregivers often gets in the way of developing self-awareness, sympathy, empathy, impulse control, and self-motivation. But parents, teachers, and other caregivers can help in breaking these patterns and interrupting the cycle of intergenerational trauma. By learning to foster strong, solidly attached, regulated relationships with their children, parents can support them in navigating their pain and in forging the critical links that children need to feel fully alive and connected.

In this book, my colleague Dafna Lender teaches clinicians, therapists, and mental health professionals how to equip parents with this power. Dafna's framework, integrative attachment family therapy (IAFT), uses the power of neuroplasticity to provide parents and children with new experiences of safety and connection that shift trauma-informed relationships. It offers a powerful mental health intervention that can help families to heal.

I first met Dafna in 2015 at the Lifespan Integration Conference in Los Angeles, where she and Phyllis Booth presented on their work in Theraplay. The videos they shared spoke to me deeply because they showed Dafna and Phyllis facilitating the type of attuned, responsive, playful parent-child interactions that can lead to secure attachment and building resilience. I asked them to present at my International Trauma Conference the subsequent year. This was the beginning of a series of presentations and trainings Dafna gave at the Trauma Research Foundation.

The trainings Dafna has offered at TRF have been focused on preventing intergenerational trauma through direct parent-child work in which attachment-based play and interventions help parents to build a more empathic understanding and communication style with their children. Dafna has been particularly critical to our development of a parent curriculum called "Inspired Parenting," a free online program that helps parents learn how to parent from an attachment- and trauma-informed perspective.

The crux of the program emphasizes playfulness, connection, and meeting the child at their developmental level rather than their chronological age. It also offers critical help to parents in resolving their own past attachment trauma issues. If parents and therapists follow Dafna's guidance, they can make significant progress in reducing attachment trauma in future generations.

The book you now hold in your hands offers therapists and mental health professionals a chance to integrate Dafna's knowledge and insight into their clinical work. IAFT, a multidimensional framework for healing and strengthening attachment issues in the parent-child relationship, uses the power of play to access the nonverbal, nonconscious energy exchanged between parent and child. When the parent and child learn to attune to and be in sync with each other, the child feels a sense of safety that enables their connection to self and other.

The focus of IAFT is on teaching parents how to provide their children with a holding environment and a predictable, competent, and safe relationship where connections can flourish—an environment in which children learn to understand, trust, and ultimately regulate themselves. Experiences that directly contradict the helplessness, rage, and collapse that are part of their response to trauma can transform both children and adults. By offering a framework and a set of tools for healing the connection between parents and children, IAFT can meaningfully contribute to healing in our human community.

—**Bessel van der Kolk, MD,** professor of psychiatry at the Boston University School of Medicine, president of the Trauma Research Foundation, and #1 *New York Times* best-selling author of *The Body Keeps the Score*

Introduction

I remember the first day I saw attachment theory truly applied in clinical practice. It happened in the hallway of the child welfare agency where I was working as a new social worker. The police had just dropped off four-year-old Timmy and his two older brothers on the agency's doorstep. The boys had seen their mother die after being stabbed by her boyfriend. When they arrived, the older brothers looked shocked and disoriented, but they could at least nod their heads to questions like "Do you want a drink?" or "Can you come sit here?" Timmy, in contrast, was a shell of a child, stooped low and on the verge of collapse. He found the first couch in the lobby and balled himself into it like the smallest water bug coiled against a predator. Various people tried to approach him, asking if he could sit up, telling him there was a nice playroom with toys down the hall. Timmy stayed in his tight ball. The minutes passed. No one could elicit the slightest response from him. The only indication that he was alive was a shallow rise and fall of his tiny back as he breathed.

That day, our clinical consultant, Sandy, happened to be in the building. Witnessing this distressing scene, Sandy approached Timmy. She crouched down by his side and started singing in a soft, rhythmic way: "Timmy, Timmy, you are here today. What did you bring with you? You are here today." She hummed a few more bars: "Oh, I see you brought your elbow. It's a fine elbow. I bet it's a pointy one, like mine. Or maybe it's soft or squishy. I don't know. I'm going to check and see." Sandy reached her hand out and gently cupped Timmy's elbow. Timmy didn't budge, but he didn't recoil either. "Oh!" Sandy whispered with a bit of energy. "It's pointy. Just like mine!" She continued this way, gently cooing at Timmy, finding ways to connect with him physically, like drawing a shape on his back and seeing if she could feel all five toes within his Spider-Man sneakers. She asked him to wiggle his toes if he had all five of them, and then Timmy wiggled them ever so slightly. Sandy exclaimed quietly but with energy, "You do! You do have five toes in there!"

I saw Timmy's breathing slow and deepen. After about five minutes, he agreed to sit up, and Sandy offered him a piggyback ride to the playroom, where he could be more comfortable. She told him there were blankets and places to hide there. He climbed on her back and hid his face in her hair. She carried him down the hall, walking a steady, firm pace, humming her Timmy song all the way. Once in the playroom, Timmy accepted a drink and slowly oriented to his new surroundings. All the while, Sandy sat next to him with her hand on his back or cupping her hands around his.

I watched this scene in awe. Sandy had never met Timmy before. How did she know how to reach this little person? How did she have the courage to approach him so closely? And how could Timmy trust a stranger after what he'd just been through?

Neuroscientist and trauma researcher Stephen Porges knows.

According to Porges's polyvagal theory (2015), Timmy was reassured by Sandy's prosodic, rhythmic voice; her lack of hesitation to connect with him through touch at the right moment, with the right pacing; her focus on the here and now of his physical presence on this earth; her complete confidence in his humanity; and her lack of fear about what had happened to him. That's what brought Timmy out of his paralysis: nonverbal communication that transmitted the message to his brain, "You're safe, you're safe."

I thought it was magic. I thought Sandy was a magician, and my mind locked onto her like a person possessed. I wanted to be like her. But how? My great fortune was that right in Chicago where I lived was The Theraplay Institute, where Sandy had been trained. Theraplay®, created by Phyllis Booth and Ann Jernberg (2010), is based on the attachment work of John Bowlby (1983) and two theories promoted by Donald Winnicott (1968): his holding environment—the idea that good parents and therapists can create a nurturing emotional environment for children—and his theory that play is the best way a child can experience their true self. Theraplay emphasizes all the nonverbal elements of Sandy's engagement with Timmy—behaviors that, in a split second, tell a child that they're safe: the rhythmic, prosodic voice; the curious, open face; the smooth, coordinated gestures; the touch and playfulness. I jumped at the opportunity to take the training, and it dramatically influenced my work and changed my career.

Integrative Attachment Family Therapy

Today, I practice integrative attachment family therapy (IAFT), a multidimensional framework I've developed to heal and strengthen attachment issues in the parent-child relationship. IAFT is informed first and foremost by Theraplay. It is also informed by polyvagal theory and dyadic developmental psychotherapy (DDP), as well as by intersubjectivity and interpersonal neurobiology research. This discourse is body-specific and based in the nonverbal, nonconscious energy exchanged between parent, child, and therapist.

IAFT is a powerful intervention that heals many common problems for which parents bring their children to therapy, including lying, controlling and manipulative behaviors, defiance, arguing, frequent tantrums, and seemingly pointless disobedience, as well as more internalizing symptoms such as indifference, disconnection, boredom, and depression. This approach addresses such a wide array of behaviors and symptoms because it treats the underlying cause: a basic problem in the parent-child relationship where the child does not feel deeply understood or accepted. IAFT helps clinicians uncover the reasons for the misalignment between parent and child so they can guide families toward looking at the source of the issues rather than the superficial behaviors. More importantly, this approach provides concrete tools and interventions that actually address and correct the issues so families can transform into happy and well-functioning environments in which children can grow.

At the core of the IAFT approach is the notion that the parent-child relationship is the key to creating the platform for the child's healthy emotional development. Treatment must start with the parent, as the parent is the main source of the child's guidance and comfort, the lens through which they interpret the world. Too often, clinicians shy away from working directly with parents because they come with a host of defenses and dysfunctions that are off-putting and complex. However, creating a strong alliance with the parents and then doing the deep therapeutic work throughout the therapy process is the crucial, and often missing, piece of therapeutic work with children.

In this book, I provide an overview of the IAFT approach for any clinicians, child welfare workers, or educators who want to stop viewing the child as the problem and who want to start effectively alleviating suffering by treating the parent-child relationship. This book is for the clinician who has been dedicated to improving children's mental health but has felt discouraged by the obstacles that parents or the mental health system has put in their way. It is for the clinician who enjoys working with children but has sensed that something is missing from their toolbox to create deep, positive change for their young clients. It is for the clinician who feels that the nonverbal, moment-to-moment attunement between the parent and their child is most important but who has not yet discovered how to focus on that deeper, physiologic level.

What Is in This Book

In the chapters that follow, I explain the foundational theories and concepts that inform IAFT. In chapter 1, I introduce three key tools that IAFT uses to promote attachment security, resiliency, and a sense of self: play, parent work, and deliberate dialogue. I then provide two case overviews to illustrate how these concepts can look in practice with two seemingly different presenting problems.

In chapter 2, I discuss the influence of polyvagal theory, and the social engagement system (SES) in particular, on the energetic work of IAFT. Polyvagal theory explains the impact of the vagus nerve on our bodies and minds, offering an accessible and useful explanation for how and why people respond in suboptimal, as well as optimal, ways to stressful situations. The SES provides the means for understanding and strengthening our nonconscious capacity for connecting with others. In IAFT, polyvagal theory helps to explain the body's nonverbal, nonconscious responses to external stimuli and experiences, and the SES indicates opportunities for regulation and connection.

In chapter 3, I discuss Theraplay and DDP. Developed by clinical psychologist Daniel A. Hughes in response to the profound needs of foster and adopted children, DDP's tools provide support to children who have a diffuse and disorganized sense of self due to weak attachment bonds. It engages the parent-child dyad in exercises and conversations designed to provoke and support the process of the child's discovery of self.

In chapter 4, I turn from inputs to outputs and discuss the preparation that therapists can complete to effectively implement IAFT. I introduce and offer a sample of the letter to a potential client explaining the IAFT approach and parental expectations. I also introduce and explain activities that will help you prepare yourself and your own SES to implement IAFT. These activities are similar to—and sometimes the same as—the activities you will complete with your clients or that you will ask your clients to complete.

Chapter 5 provides an overview of a typical IAFT cycle, as well as a rationale for the timing and importance of each phase and its associated activities. Chapters 6, 7, and 8 guide you through the main phases of an IAFT cycle: dyad assessment, working with parents, and working with children. Finally, chapter 9 explores challenges that commonly arise in IAFT and provides potential solutions.

Taken together, the conceptual chapters in the first half of the book provide the foundation for the practical chapters in the second half. It is my hope that when you finish reading this book, you will feel the same sense of the magic of connection that I came to know—a magic that I continue to feel with my clients every day.

1

Foundations of Integrative Attachment Family Therapy

Although I use a variety of tools to implement the IAFT framework, the tools themselves are not the key to its efficacy. The key is connection. A strong connection facilitates attachment security, the child's resiliency, and the child's sense of self. However, connection cannot happen without an enveloping sense of safety. Accordingly, IAFT promotes the sense of safety that fosters connection—connection between the therapist and the child, connection between the therapist and the parent, and, most importantly, connection between the child and the parent. Each of these connections, when forged through the therapist's whole self, strengthens attachment security and the child's sense of self. How? By challenging and changing the child's inner working model and implicit relational knowing, their nonconscious expectation of what will come from interacting with another human being.

In traditional discourse, characterized by Bowlby (1983), patterns of attachment are established during a child's infancy when a parent responds in an attuned way (or not) to their baby's signals. These patterns turn into schemas that are neurologically set in the brain over the first three years. The more they are repeated, the more they are reinforced. The repeated schemas turn into the child's internal working model—their mental representation of relationships—based on their primary attachment relationship, which helps them make sense of all other relationships. Attachment patterns are typically considered adequate when characterized by open, responsive interactions and functional communications. Inadequate attachments are characterized by closed, nonresponsive interactions and dysfunctional communications.

In the language of IAFT, adequate attachment is characterized by a parent and child who are regulated and in sync with one another; inadequate attachment is characterized by a parent and child who are dysregulated and out of sync. Attachment and the reciprocal influence of the internal working model are an ongoing and dynamic process that manifests in different relationships in different ways at different times. Consequently, attachment patterns can change and impact individuals, both for the worse and for the better. An attachment pattern may be adequate for long periods of time, but a challenging life event or a new relationship can disrupt the pattern. Or an attachment pattern may be inadequate but manifest in ways that obscure the attachment issue at the root of the problem.

Regardless, when attachment is inadequate, relationships suffer. If the primary caregiving relationship weakens or deteriorates, the individuals—and the individuals' behaviors—usually suffer too. A parent in a relationship characterized by insecure or inadequate attachment may behave coldly or punitively. A child in this type of relationship may behave defiantly, aggressively, or profoundly apathetically.

Although it isn't always easy to know when a behavior is an attachment issue, we can use the following diagnostic questions as a guide when observing and assessing the parent-child dyad:

1. Does the child feel able to say how they feel without fearing that the parent will respond with recrimination, anger, disgust, or rejection, or will take the child's feelings or expression of ideas as a betrayal or a personal injury to them?

2. Does the child feel that the parent is sufficiently present and attuned to protect them and to stand by their side, even when the parent may feel extreme anger at the child?

3. Does the child feel special in their parent's eyes, and that their parent is uniquely interested in them, just because they are them and not because they fulfill a parental need, such as pride or validation?

When any of the preceding questions are answered with a no, IAFT can help. Its framework reflects my understanding that the connection between parent and child, which is expressed by the verbal and nonverbal elements of the parent-child relationship, is often the root of the child's behavior problems and struggles. In this way, IAFT contradicts individualist assumptions that a child is a bounded vessel in which problems are contained. Children are not discrete individuals in IAFT. Rather, a child exists *in relationship to* their caregiver. The point of focus is therefore the parent-child dyad and its connectedness or disconnectedness. Additionally, whereas traditional therapists frequently lean on the child's capacity to change, focusing on "fixing" the child—fixing their anger issues or fixing their defiance, for instance—an IAFT therapist leans instead on the *parent's* capacity to change.

Working closely with parent and child, separately and together, IAFT therapists help foster the aforementioned *attachment security*. This kind of security results from a parent's ability to support their child's exploration of negative affect and to tolerate and accept that their child is different from them. With attachment security, a parent can respect their child's preferences, ideas, and desires—without compromising their own sense of self or their needs and boundaries, and even when they may not be pleased with or like their child's choices. Attachment security happens when a parent is able to avoid sending both verbal and nonverbal signals of disdain, disapproval, and anxiety, and when they are able to verbally and nonverbally show their child that they enjoy and admire them just as they are.

The parent's ability to convey attachment security is the foundation for the child's developing *resiliency*, or the ability to cope with tough situations by adapting, to ask for help from others when feeling vulnerable, to use positive self-talk, and to find creative solutions to seemingly huge obstacles. When the parent is able to respond to their child in ways that support attachment security, the child can use the parent as a platform for exploring and developing their own identity, thoughts, wishes, opinions, and sources of pleasure. The child can seek advice and guidance from the parent, using them as a sounding board. The child can avoid feeling alone or ashamed when they do something wrong or struggle with a dilemma.

Through developing and strengthening attachment security and resilience, the IAFT framework also fosters the child's *sense of self*. In fact, a child inevitably develops a sense of self when they are supported and accepted in the ways described above. This sense of self is a largely nonconscious sense—it's the voice that lives within us—and it, too, is dynamic. For example, when a young child is shamed by their parent for doing something normal, such as getting dirty or crying loudly, their sense of self can become disorganized and weak. Fortunately, however, it can also become organized and strong. A strong sense of self can help us make choices about how we express ourselves, how we spend our time, and the kinds of people we choose as friends.

Many therapeutic practices approach and treat issues of attachment, as well as resiliency and a cohesive sense of self. In addition to Theraplay, prominent examples include child-parent psychotherapy (Lieberman & Van Horn, 2011) and the circle of security (Zanetti et al., 2011). However, the IAFT approach is different. Whereas the preceding approaches typically focus on one or two components of secure attachment, IAFT promotes attachment security, resiliency, and a sense of self through a fuller, more dynamic set of attachment-promoting tools: play, parent work, and deliberate dialogue.

In each of these areas, the IAFT therapist focuses not only on verbal communication between the parent and child but, crucially, on their nonverbal communication. Verbal communication, the heart of many traditional therapies, involves the words that a parent and child use to communicate with each other. Nonverbal communication, the heart of IAFT, includes the body gestures, posture, tone of voice, and facial expressions that give meaning to those words. Nonverbal communication is typically nonconscious, which means it offers a powerful access point through which suffering can be understood and alleviated. By focusing on nonverbal communication, IAFT offers therapists strategies for peering into the difficulties and power struggles that are often missed or unaddressed in session because they are not part of the conscious conversation.

Ultimately, IAFT is a critical model for helping the parent and child truly connect. Its innovative approach to a dynamic understanding of attachment, paired with its nonverbal focus, facilitates a child's ability to communicate their thoughts and feelings, while also supporting the parent's ability to show their child understanding and validation. In fact, the parent's ability to understand and validate the child's experience is the main objective of IAFT. This is what enables the strong connection that promotes attachment security, resilience, and a sense of self.

The Four Phases of IAFT

IAFT involves four phases, each focusing on a different person or dyad within the family structure. Here is an overview:

The Four Phases of IAFT

FIRST PHASE: *FOCUS ON THE PARENT*

- **Session 1:** Agreement and intake
- **Session 2:** Parental attachment history
- **Session 3:** Parent-child play assessment with the social engagement principles
- **Session 4:** Parent-only session—PACE (playfulness, acceptance, curiosity, and empathy) and deliberate dialogue role-play

SECOND PHASE: *FOCUS ON THE PARENT-CHILD DYAD*

- **Sessions 1 to 3:** Parent and child
- **Session 4:** Parent-only session

THIRD PHASE: *SPECIALIZED FOCUS ON THE PARENT*

- **Sessions 1 to 5:** Individual parent work, if necessary

FOURTH PHASE: *FOCUS ON THE SECOND PARENT*

- If necessary, repeat the previous three phases with the second parent and the child

---

Dyadic sessions are repeated in cycles of four: three dyadic sessions followed by one parent-only session, or a pause for two to five parent-only sessions, until the IAFT therapist and clients feel that some or most of the therapeutic goals have been achieved or that the opportunity for optimal progress has been met.

Let's take a look at two case overviews that show IAFT at work in child-parent situations that therapists often encounter. The first case features a so-called typical situation. Here, the child and parent are engaged in something of a power struggle: The child appears disempowered and downtrodden, while the parent appears exasperated and dismissive. Their relationship has suffered, and they are unable to effectively communicate. The second case describes a more difficult situation. Here, the child exhibits severe emotional and behavioral problems due to a history of abuse and neglect. The parent is frustrated but resigned, and the parent-child relationship has markedly and dramatically deteriorated. In both cases, there is an urgent need to work with both parent and child, as well as the parent-child dyad, to reestablish a healthy connection.

Case Overview: Matilda

First, the more typical case: 12-year-old Matilda was brought to therapy by her parents, Eric and Samantha. They were worried about Matilda because she had behavioral problems at home. Matilda was an excellent student and a star athlete. However, even though she chose to play soccer, she sometimes refused to go to practice. Her parents firmly believed that when you make a commitment to a team, you must show up for your commitment even if you "don't feel like participating." At times, they tried to drag Matilda out of her room and into the car to go to practice. They also complained that Matilda had other emotional outbursts of disrespect toward them, such as calling them names and refusing to clean her room. At other times, they noted, Matilda expressed feelings of anxiety and a sense of worthlessness.

When I met with Matilda and her parents, I quickly took note of a number of nonverbal cues. For example, Matilda sat between her parents with a stiff back and a pasted smile on her face. I asked her what she wanted help with and how she saw the problem. Matilda said that, at times, in the past weeks, she felt sad, hopeless, or overwhelmed, and that she sometimes couldn't make herself do homework. I asked her directly about the battles with her parents regarding her participation in soccer. Matilda's face flushed as she looked sideways at her parents and said, "I feel bad because I know my teammates are counting on me. Also, I told my parents I wanted to be in the competitive league, and they paid a lot of money for me to play. But I don't feel like going anymore. I know I'm letting my parents and teammates down by not showing up consistently. I sometimes just can't make myself go."

"Is it hard for you to say how you have mixed feelings and may have changed your mind about soccer? Do think there is something wrong with you that you made a commitment you can't keep?" I asked.

"*Can't* or *won't*?" Eric interjected in an urgent tone and with judgment in his eyes.

I got the strong sense that something deeper was going on between the parents and Matilda—something more than the presenting problem of Matilda sometimes being "oppositional."

In a session alone with Matilda, she presented as she did with her parents. Her polite smile barely hid her sadness. Her shoulders were hunched, and she looked immobilized. She apologized each time she was critical of her parents and thanked me repeatedly for every favorable comment I made toward her. When I told her she neither had to apologize for her feelings nor thank me for doing my job, it was as if I had disarmed her—her only coping methods appeared to be worrying about others and trying to constantly please them rather than allowing herself to feel her feelings.

In the first phase of our work, I focused on Matilda's parents, digging deeper into their background and how it related to Eric's uncompromising position on "keeping commitments." When I suggested that he put pressure on Matilda regarding soccer, he expressed that, compared to his childhood, Matilda "had it so good"—he felt she needed to learn that life is tough and that she has to work hard and not shirk her responsibilities. I learned that Eric was the son of immigrants, that his father owned a grocery store, and that Eric was expected to work there from the age of 14. I also learned that Eric's father was harsh, uncompromising, and frightening. He never praised or supported Eric, so Eric had to go it alone—work at the store and get himself through both high school and college. Eric told me with tears of anger and sadness that his dad was cruel. He said, "I didn't get any of the advantages that Matilda has. The least she can do is be grateful and appreciate all of the opportunities she has. Is that too much to ask?"

It was clear to me that the pressure applied by her parents, especially her dad, as well as Matilda's guilt-ridden presentation and oppositionality at home, constituted a relational issue. But was it an attachment issue? Yes, I believed it was. Attachment security allows a child to have conflicting feelings, to make messy choices, and to vacillate or act inconsistently without fearing that these ambivalent feelings will destroy their parents, their family, and thus themselves. Insecure attachment is often characterized by parents who become so angered by or disappointed in their child's ambivalent feelings that the child can no longer authentically or honestly express their feelings. The child must hide their feelings to maintain their relationships to their parents and their family. By doing so, the child compromises their needs so much that it significantly impacts their emotional and psychological health.

Eric's demand that Matilda be strong, his inability to tolerate Matilda's internal dilemmas, and his tendency to highlight her ingratitude are typical of dismissive adults. Given the attachment insecurity informed by this underlying dynamic, I focused our work on in vivo interactions in dyadic therapy rather than working with Matilda alone. In fact, it was the relationship between child and parent that I wanted to treat; working alone with Matilda would reinforce the identification of Matilda as the problem and the locus of change, while working with Eric and Matilda would be the most salient and powerful route to satisfying and lasting change for the family.

Consequently, after completing the first phase of work, I turned to the second phase and the parent-child dyad. Each session, we played games to establish a sense of safety, fun, and connection. Then we moved into discussing a challenging behavior or experience. I first sought to help Matilda feel safe expressing her negative feelings. I didn't want her to worry about Eric's negative reactions, or that he was going to jump in and persuade Matilda on his point of view. I also began to help Eric become aware of his nonverbal reactions, like wincing or shaking his head in response to something Matilda said. I noticed Eric's nonverbal reactions aloud, gently asking if he'd like to take a couple of deep breaths, if he'd like to shake out his shoulders, or if he'd like to take a break. Initially, Eric took this opportunity to insert his opinion. When I pointed out that, in these moments, it was important that he change his body language to facilitate Matilda feeling more at ease to speak, he began to notice his nonverbal reactions more readily.

Next, I helped Matilda develop the courage to express her mixed feelings about sports and school, as well as her anger toward her parents for constantly stressing out and yelling at her and her siblings. This work was difficult, in part, because Matilda frequently looked at her father to check if she was hurting his feelings or making him mad. I reminded Matilda that it was okay to have opinions and feelings that were uncomfortable for or displeased her father. I sometimes had to position my chair such that Matilda was looking toward me and could not easily glance sideways to gauge her father's reaction.

Once Eric was better able to neutrally listen to Matilda's feelings, and Matilda felt capable of sharing those feelings, I sought to facilitate a direct dialogue that felt regulated and safe. Using the PACE attitude—which emphasizes playfulness, acceptance, curiosity, and empathy—and deliberate dialogue (both of which will be discussed in chapter 3), we worked to help Matilda express her feelings about specific situations at home and to help her father respond with acceptance and empathy. The challenge here was in helping Eric to understand Matilda's experience of the situation and to let her know that he understood her point of view and deeply cared about her feelings. With active guidance, Eric was able to become open and empathic as he listened and connected with Matilda about her experiences.

Ultimately, Matilda was able to express that she would get very stressed before soccer games and had a hard time overcoming her anxiety. Eric was finally able to put himself in her shoes, and he seemed to understand the depths of her struggles in going to the soccer matches. From there, Eric was able to see how his lectures about being a responsible teammate and honoring commitments created a bigger conflict for Matilda. Through this work together, Eric's rigid position about Matilda's soccer commitment softened. Because he pressured her less, Matilda decided herself to finish the soccer season but was also able to say that, despite the fact that she was very good at soccer, she felt too much pressure and would not play in the subsequent season.

This case could have been dealt with in any number of ways, including cognitive behavior therapy (CBT), individual work with Matilda on coping with stress, or parental guidance focusing on setting limits with adolescents. However, by focusing on the parent-child dyad and their nonverbal interactions, by getting to know the parent's own attachment history, and by focusing on the parent's capacity to develop empathy for the child's ambivalent feelings about her choices and identity, IAFT not only helped Matilda and her father relieve the conflicts at home, but also—and more importantly—created a feeling of greater closeness and harmony between them that allowed for additional growth beyond the therapy room. Attachment security was strengthened, and Matilda was able to gain a more organized sense of self to guide decisions informed by her own feelings, rather than those of her father.

Case Overview: Natasha

This story is about a more severe case of a child with major attachment issues subsequent to trauma associated with prolonged abuse and neglect. Natasha was 13 years old when she came to visit me with Elaine, an American single mother who had adopted Natasha from Russia at age 9. Natasha had endured a very painful early life. Until age 5, she had lived with neglectful and abusive parents. Records documented that Natasha and her younger brother were found several times alone in a dirty apartment without food or heat. At age 5, she was removed from her parents' home, separated from her brother, and sent to live at her maternal aunt's home. At age 8, she was removed again due to neglect and moved to an orphanage, where she lived until the time of her adoption. During the first year after her adoption, Natasha related stories about scary, drunk men coming in and out of the apartment where she had lived, lots of yelling, and the police arriving many times to break up arguments. By her second year in America, Natasha no longer spoke about her previous life in Russia; she claimed to have no memory of her parents or her aunt, and only vague memories of her brother.

When I met with Elaine for the first time, she described Natasha's behavior as a frightening combination of icy disengagement and fiery rage. Her default mode of disengagement seemed almost robotic: She'd answer in apathetic grunts to even benign questions like "Where would you like to go for dinner?" and frequently retreated to her room. Natasha seemed annoyed by Elaine's overtures for closeness and refused to give her any details about how her school day went, how soccer practice went, and so forth. One time, when Elaine tried to raise Natasha's pants leg to check out what seemed like a nasty bruise from being kicked on the soccer field, Natasha pulled her leg away reflexively and said with disgust, "Ew, you're gross."

This rejection was coupled with a rageful side that would emerge full-blown without warning at seemingly trivial things. For example, Elaine declined to buy Natasha some expensive jeans after having just purchased three nice shirts for her. Natasha, having seemed calm a moment earlier, started shrieking, "You never get me what I want! You don't love me! You just adopted me so you could be mean to me!" Her cutting words were accompanied by hot, gushing, angry tears. Natasha could quickly become aggressive, including flinging papers off the desk and threatening to throw a paperweight at her mother's head. These scenes would usually end with Natasha running to her room, slamming the door so hard the frame of the house shook, and crying piteously by herself. If Elaine tried to knock gently and enter, Natasha would snarl viciously, "Get out of here! I hate you!"

By the time this dyad reached me, I sensed that this mother was living in a state of traumatic stress. Elaine relayed that she could not remember events from one day to the next because she dreaded interacting with her daughter. She felt an impending sense of doom. Elaine wept quietly as she mumbled to me through shameful tears, "I would give her back if I could, but I have nowhere to send her." Such was the voice of utter despair and terror that Elaine had internalized mothering Natasha.

The feeling I got from my first encounter with Natasha was that she was not actually there—she was physically present but psychologically hidden. She was withdrawn and distant, in a state of chronic dissociation. She had closed herself up a long time ago. Based on her history, Natasha probably used disengagement and avoidance as an attachment strategy, trying to suppress her needs. In polyvagal terms (which we will discuss in chapter 2), she had likely been in a dorsal vagal state—a shut-off mode—from early infancy. On top of the abuse and neglect from her birth family, the stress of moving into an orphanage and being adopted overseas at an older age likely damaged Natasha's capacity to open up or consider trusting even the most caring, attuned, and responsive parent.

Natasha was a true case of the conceptual diagnosis of developmental trauma disorder, coined and developed by Bessel van der Kolk (2014). Developmental trauma disorder describes childhood trauma, such as chronic abuse, neglect, or other harsh adversity, that takes place in the child's home. When a child is exposed to overwhelming stress and their caregiver does not help reduce this stress, or is possibly the cause of the stress, the child experiences developmental trauma. The effects of abuse and neglect from a caregiver—the person who is by definition the one that a baby is supposed to rely on when in need of comfort—causes such a deep disruption in the child's development as to impede every area of their growth, from the physical to the intellectual to the psychological, behavioral, emotional, and relational.

My first task, then, was to communicate to Natasha that she was safe—safe enough to peek out from her protective state and see that maybe there could be something to motivate an effort at connection. I had to reach the part of Natasha's brain that recognized safety and another's genuine desire to discover her. Given her disinterest, I sensed that talking and asking questions would fail, as would initiating any activities that asked for her overt cooperation. I suspected the more lively attachment-based games would be more likely to awaken Natasha's need and desire to connect.

At the same time, I had to help Elaine put into context Natasha's response to Elaine's attempts to parent her. Elaine was so despondent and traumatized by Natasha's responses that she had lost her sense of hope and meaning in life. I needed to explain to her the impact of developmental trauma on a family, helping her to depersonalize her current experience of feeling so painfully and personally rejected. I also needed to inquire into Elaine's childhood experiences with her parents, to understand whether her own childhood wounds were nonconsciously playing out in her dynamics with Natasha, impeding their connection and trust. I would then have to work on bringing Natasha and Elaine together in simple, face-to-face activities that were very low stakes and generally pleasurable.

Only after this work could I help Natasha come to terms with what had happened to her. My goal, facilitated by the IAFT framework and IAFT activities, was to help Elaine, as Natasha's current attachment figure, be able to support and bear witness to Natasha's story with acceptance and empathy. Many parents have a hard time doing this because they want to reassure or rescue their child from painful thoughts and feelings. They may downplay the past or try to argue with their child about their perceptions. Parents of traumatized children may do this because they feel pain when considering the horror their children went through and want to minimize the impact of the trauma on the family's life. However, the simple joys of connection are linked to past traumas and painful stories. By facilitating the expression of both, IAFT helps parents like Elaine honor their place in their child's narrative and make sense of how difficult events have shaped their child's current functioning and sense of self. This work strengthens attachment security.

With Natasha and Elaine, I began this work when Natasha came into a session looking at the ground and picking the polish from her nails. Rather than starting to talk about their relationship, I surprised Natasha by asking, "Do you have strong arm muscles?" She looked puzzled. I turned to Elaine and asked, "Is it okay if I check how strong your daughter is?" Natasha immediately looked at her mom and then at me. She looked genuinely curious. I sat up a little and opened my eyes wider to respond to her curiosity.

"Sure," Elaine responded.

"Okay, Natasha, I'm going to have you punch a hole in my newspaper with your strong muscles." I reached for a stack of old newspapers in the bag of supplies at my side. I separated out one big sheet and spread it open. I then asked Natasha, "Are you right- or left-handed?" She lifted her left hand. "Wow! You're left-handed? I'm a lefty in sports! That makes us the same!" I asked her to make a fist with her left hand. She produced a very tight fist, and I cradled it with both my hands, looked her squarely in the eyes, and said with a resonant voice, "Ooh, that is a good fist." Her glance back looked focused and intent. I picked up the sheet of newspaper and held it out in front of me. "Okay, now, with this fist, I want you to punch a hole right here in the center of my newspaper when I say, 'one, two, three, *punch.*'" I pointed right to the center. "Now, I have my arms out, so you won't have to worry about hurting me when you punch the paper," I explained. Natasha nodded cooperatively as she poised to respond to the signal. "One, two, three, *punch!*" I said with vigor. Natasha threw a precise, purposeful fist, and I simultaneously pulled at each side of the newspaper. It tore in half cleanly and with a resounding *pop*.

Natasha looked stunned and impressed. I mirrored her face precisely. "Wow!" I exclaimed, and Natasha glanced sideways toward her mom, giggling at what she had done. Elaine looked back at Natasha with pride and recognition. Natasha leaned toward her mom's arm and rested her head there for a moment. She then sat erect again, and we repeated the process a second time, and a third, and a fourth. Each time we set up the game, I looked at Natasha and she at me with eyes that signaled, *something good is about to happen*. And when she punched, and I ripped the paper in concert, Natasha repeatedly looked at her mom and giggled like a baby.

Elaine, too, opened her eyes wide and gave out an admiring "Wow!" Natasha's laugh was so genuine, and I could tell that Elaine was both pleased and taken aback to hear her daughter's laughter: "I love to hear you laugh. That's the best sound in the world!"

We continued these types of playful, surprising games to get around Natasha's defenses. Games, in the context of IAFT, help to bring out the spontaneous joy associated with simple playful activities. We will return to games and activities in chapter 6, where I use the example of Natasha and Elaine to explain observation and assessment. Every time we played, Natasha became a softer, more present person. She responded not only to me in this way, but also to her mother.

While we made progress in our sessions, outside the sessions, Elaine could not always see the changes occurring in her daughter. She indicated that she still felt a paralyzing dread when approaching Natasha. She described feeling ineffectual and unable to connect at home. When I shared my own observations of Natasha opening up toward her, Elaine suggested that Natasha was perhaps "faking it." At the time, it shocked me to hear Elaine say this. She said it so matter-of-factly that I realized we were worlds apart in our perspectives. It was so clear to me that Natasha's responses to her mom were genuinely joyful and connected. However, when I reflected on it, I saw that part of the reason Elaine couldn't believe that Natasha was genuinely engaging with her was based on the degree to which she had shut herself off from feeling anything remotely hopeful about Natasha. She was afraid she'd be painfully rejected yet again.

In the next phase of work, I asked Elaine to come in for a series of parent-only meetings. In one of them, I cued up a segment of the last dyadic session, which I had videotaped. In this segment, a particularly moving interaction occurred between Elaine and her daughter. The game was Slippery Slip. Natasha and Elaine sat face-to-face on the floor. Elaine used hand lotion to make her hands slippery. She then held Natasha's hands and leaned back, trying at the same time to hold on to Natasha's hands. Naturally, there was a gradual and then sudden slipping away that ended with a dramatic falling backward. In the clip, Elaine and Natasha held hands—both were poised in identical postures, eyes wide open, in anticipation for the action to begin. Elaine began to say dramatically, "Ohhh nooo . . . I'm slipping awaaayyyyy!" In the same rhythm, Natasha let out a rolling giggle until they both exploded in laughter as they let go. Elaine leaned all the way back to the floor and rested there for a moment. Natasha had leaned back but then sprang back up and was immediately ready for more. She had been locked in on her mother's gaze, and when it was momentarily lost, she yearned to get it back. Natasha extended her arms out fully and, like a baby, clapped them together three times and squealed, "Come on, Mom!"

The first time Elaine watched this clip, she was mesmerized but also in a bit of disbelief. "What do you see, Elaine?" I asked.

"I don't know," she said with searching in her eyes. "Can I watch it again?"

I played it for her again. This time, Elaine reflected, "It looks like she is really having fun with me."

"Yes, Elaine, she really enjoys playing with you. Did you see her reach her arms out to you? How do you feel when you see that?"

"I want to believe she needs me, but part of me still thinks she is faking," she said.

"Oh, I understand. You have been through so much with Natasha that part of you is hesitant to believe," I matched her hesitant voice. "And maybe it's not all the time, but I think something is changing between you two. Part of Natasha doesn't want a mom, and she lets you know that loud and clear, but there is another part of her, the part we see here, that is saying, 'I want you, Mom!' You know how I know? I can see it in her eyes, how she looks into your gaze in anticipation, how she synchronizes to your movement, how her giggle crescendos to your 'ohhh nooo.' She's communicating to you with her body, and those signals can't be faked." Elaine looked moved as she let this new perspective settle on her. This was the beginning of real therapeutic movement between the dyad.

My understanding of the change process that occurred between Natasha and Elaine was that the nonverbal interactions, which were prompted by games and therefore not as controlled as normal day-to-day interactions, facilitated an opening of each of the dyad's attachment system to pick up previously unrecognizable positive cues. The recognition that it could be safe and pleasurable to interact seeped into their home life. Elaine reported that Natasha now purposefully sought her out. She described one incident where Natasha emerged from her room and nonchalantly asked Elaine to make her some ramen noodles. Elaine was more than happy to oblige but asked in amusement, "How come you're not making them yourself?" To which Natasha responded, "They taste better when you make them."

Feeling that Natasha trusted her and wanted to be in her presence, Elaine's sense of confidence in her role as a mother blossomed. In therapy, she was now able to be present and supportive in a way that was much more palpable to her daughter. In one particularly difficult session, we were exploring a vivid nightmare that Natasha had had the night before. In it, Elaine had died in a car crash, and Natasha had to move to a stranger's home in California. She had to take a bus by herself and didn't know how to get there. Natasha could barely talk during the session, speaking in a weak whisper. But she allowed her mom to recount the dream as Natasha had relayed it in the middle of the night. Elaine used a rich, tender voice to describe not only the dream but how she had found Natasha looking panicked and grief-stricken. She expressed how hard that must have been for Natasha as she awoke in alarm.

"It happens a lot," Natasha mumbled.

"I know," Elaine said. "I hear you at night when you call out in your sleep. I always want to go in and comfort you and let you know that I'm here for you."

"You're doing that now, Elaine," I noted. Natasha laid her head on a pillow, leaning in her mom's direction. Elaine reached out and put her hand on Natasha's thick blonde hair and began to tenderly stroke her head. The three of us sat there in silence for several minutes. Natasha's breathing became deeper and more rhythmic. As I looked at Elaine, I saw an expression of sadness and the warmth of a mother with a steadfast dedication to comforting her child.

These transformative events were the beginning of a long series of cascading, positive events for Natasha and Elaine that led to Natasha's growing ability to go to her mom for comfort, connection, and pleasure. The interventions had to access deep, nonconscious levels of both Natasha's and Elaine's soul because that was where the damage had occurred—and where the potential for healing lay.

The Power of IAFT

As illustrated by these cases, IAFT strengthens the attachment relationship through play, parent work, and deliberate dialogue. Play, as it is informed by attachment figures like Winnicott (1968) and Colwyn Trevarthen (Trevarthen & Aitkin, 2001), as well as Virginia Axline's (1969) work and Theraplay, offers a vehicle for creating the fun and lighthearted moments that enable nonverbal connection and facilitate the soothing and caring interactions that promote attachment.

IAFT's emphasis on parent work helps parents reflect on their own attachment history and understand how their past experiences may be affecting their relationship with their child. In the example of Matilda and Eric, for instance, Eric had to become aware that his tendency to criticize Matilda was informed by his feelings of shame and anger about not being good enough for his own father. This kind of insight can offer the parent new ways to interact with their child. When Eric understood that he was seeking to somehow justify his father's cruel behavior by imposing his own rigid and exacting rules on Matilda, he was able to understand his behavior and to express compassion for himself—and therefore choose to separate himself from this critical and harsh position and choose a gentler approach.

Deliberate dialogue, supported with the PACE attitude, helps the parent and child engage in new conversations around sometimes difficult topics. When a parent and child have to talk about emotionally charged subjects, such as arguments they have had or feelings of pain, rejection, or anger, they often feel scared and do not know how to navigate the conversation. They may turn to familiar patterns of communicating, such as defending themselves, dismissing or minimizing the other person's feelings, or trying to reassure the other person. The PACE attitude and deliberate dialogue provide specific directions for navigating these tough conversations. The structure is particularly useful to teach because it helps the parent learn how to get to the deeper issue that is at the heart of conflicts while ensuring they communicate to their child that they hear and understand their child's experiences.

The play, parent work, and deliberate dialogue that characterize IAFT rigorously serve safety, connection, and attachment. However, it is not the case that the parent and child play together and suddenly all is well. Nor is it the case that the parent, after reflecting on their own early experiences, is instantly better able to relate to their child. And, of course, deliberate dialogue takes time to learn and to influence the dyad's day-to-day conversations and interactions. Play, parent work, and deliberate dialogue work at a deeper level. They facilitate connection and deepen attachment by strengthening the nonverbal communication that promotes attunement, co-regulation, and intersubjectivity in a healthy parent-child dyad.

2

Connection, Polyvagal Theory, and the Social Engagement System

The straightforward goal of IAFT is to first communicate a sense of safety in session so as to establish and strengthen the connection between a parent and child. As I have discussed, a strong connection facilitates attachment security, the child's resiliency, and the child's sense of self. But first we must define a *strong connection*. While *connection* can describe a number of affiliations, in IAFT, the strong connection in a functioning parent-child dyad is characterized by attunement, co-regulation, and intersubjectivity.

The Basis of Connection

Attunement

Attunement refers to the nonconscious, nonverbal ability to pick up on another person's feelings and sensations. It is perhaps easiest to see at work in parents of babies: Parents typically understand their baby's nonverbal signals through careful, but not necessarily conscious, study. They not only observe whether their baby is screaming, wiggling, squirming, or squealing but also consider the color and temperature of their baby's skin, the fluidity of their baby's movements, the dilation or constriction of their baby's pupils, and the rhythm of their baby's breathing. Because babies are nonverbal, parents must sense these subtle signs to understand how their baby is doing and to anticipate what their baby might need next. In fact, this sensing *is* attunement.

Although attunement is an important facet of the parent-child relationship all on its own, it serves a crucial function: Attunement helps the child develop empathy. Attunement facilitates a sense of two people *being with* each other, or what I also call being *in sync* with each other. It permits emotional communication and connection, and it therefore creates the capacity of empathizing with another person (Siegel, 2020).

Co-regulation

Connection is also characterized by co-regulation. This refers to the phenomenon whereby a parent, having registered their child's experience through the mechanism of attunement, nonconsciously engages in behaviors that enable them to join their own energy with the child's energy. As with the being-with of attunement, co-regulation signals to the child, *I'm together with you; I register you.* In addition to this nonverbal message of support, co-regulation refers to the parent's simultaneous ability, also nonconscious, to understand whether they should match their child's energy, or increase or decrease their own affect, to help regulate their child. We see a powerful example of nonconscious co-regulation in the infant's earliest moments: When a newborn is placed on their parent's chest, the baby's heart rate begins to synchronize with the caregiver holding them. The parent's and the child's heart co-regulate.

Co-regulation occurs when a parent responds to the child's level of physical or emotional arousal and modulates it in a way that maintains or, if necessary, returns that arousal to a comfortable level. This comfortable level is also known as the child's window of tolerance (Siegel, 2020). When a parent co-regulates, they first attune to their child's state. They then make a largely nonconscious decision about whether to simply notice the moment or to join in it, communicating, *I see you; I'm with you* and simultaneously increasing the affect (in cases where the state is pleasurable and appropriate) or decreasing the affect (in cases where the physiologic state is one of distress or discomfort, or inappropriate). Next, they use their facial expressions, gestures, posture, eye contact, and tone of voice to co-regulate with their child.

Co-regulation builds through a child's interactions with caregivers that are predictable, responsive, and supportive. As with attunement, co-regulation is important all on its own; however, a parent-child relationship in which the parent and child capably co-regulate also fosters the child's self-regulation.

Repeated positive experiences of this interactive process lead to a greater ability to self-regulate.

Primary Intersubjectivity

Intersubjectivity, the third element of a strong connection, is related to attunement and co-regulation and describes a person's capacity for understanding what goes on in the mind of another person with whom they are in a relationship. Our capacity for intersubjectivity depends on our experience of feeling deeply known and connected to another person, often our primary attachment figure. Having developed this capacity, we are able to be aware that we know the people with whom we are in a relationship. Thus, intersubjectivity is a shared state of feelings and actions that results when two people sense that they really understand each other (Trevarthen & Aitken, 2001). It's important to note that our capacity for intersubjectivity is not predicated on the depth of the relationship. In fact, a relationship does not have to be particularly deep or sustained for its participants to experience intersubjectivity—we can experience it with the clerk at the grocery store! This is because, according to Daniel Stern, intersubjectivity is a little like saying, "I know what you are feeling" and "I know that you know that I know what you are feeling, and vice versa" (Stern, 2004, p. 81).

Intersubjectivity begins to develop in infancy. However, we are initially not aware of this joint state of consciousness. Rather, this awareness emerges over time, typically over the course of the first two years, as the child's brain develops in response to sensitive and attuned interactions with their caregivers. Such parent-child interactions happen countless times in a day and are the platform for the baby's emerging conscious awareness of the type of connection they seek from other people.

Attunement, co-regulation, and intersubjectivity are important to a variety of therapies. However, IAFT considers them the foundational supports of the strongly connected parent-child dyad. When any one of these capacities is weak or broken, the parent-child dyad is no longer connected and can no longer function. This is why the IAFT therapist's first task is not to seek to understand what the presenting problem is, when it started, in what contexts it is most pronounced, or how it impairs functioning. Instead, we seek to first understand the physiologic experience of safety and connection in the parent-child dyad. Everything else, including the answers to questions about presenting issues, is just conscious articulation—a story—sitting on top of the more primary disruption.

Of course, stories can clarify, but they can also obstruct and distort. This is why the IAFT therapist uses polyvagal theory, and the social engagement system in particular, to observe, assess, and ultimately modulate what the child, in the context of the parent-child dyad, experiences on the most basic level of being.

Polyvagal Theory and the Social Engagement System

Polyvagal theory and its associated social engagement system (SES) help us understand ourselves and our clients according to the ways we assess and respond to danger and safety. In fact, humans are constantly physiologically scanning, assessing, and responding to potential dangers on an organismic, physiologic level. This ongoing nonconscious effort is the reason why, in IAFT, we do not only consider what a parent or child says, or how they describe their intentions, or even their most overt behaviors. We also consider—and center—their nonverbal, nonconscious communications. We perceive this as the wavelength on which a person vibrates, and in session, we consider how each member of a parent-child dyad vibrates, as well as how these wavelengths match up and interact with one another.

IAFT situates this energetic work within the body-specific discourse of polyvagal theory and the mechanisms of the SES. Many therapists already understand and situate the body according to similar neurologic models, such as the neurosequential model of therapeutics (NMT; Perry & Dobson, 2013) or the window of tolerance (Siegel, 2020). Both of these models developed out of therapeutic work with individuals who had experienced trauma. NMT proposes a chronological approach to neurological development that helps therapists diagnose the age of trauma occurrence and determine body-specific interventions appropriate to that neurological age. If, for example, a client was neglected in early infancy and did not have the kinds of sensory experiences that babies need in the first months of life, NMT might guide a therapeutic intervention such as swimming or karate. Or, for someone who experienced early abuse and associates touch by another person as harmful or frightening, NMT might recommend massage or therapeutic horseback riding.

Siegel's window of tolerance proposes that the extent to which a person responds to the normal ebbs and flows of life depends on the level of arousal within their nervous system. According to his model, there are three different zones of arousal in which a person might be functioning: an optimal zone of arousal, a hypoaroused zone in which they are shut down or collapsed, and a hyperaroused zone in which they are keyed up and overwhelmed. These three zones offer a neurological perspective that suggests that problematic behaviors are not willful or intentional and that the remedy cannot therefore be cognitive or based on morality, but instead must be somatic and based on the senses and sensory input.

Polyvagal theory is not a radical departure from these theories and models. It also offers a neurophysiological basis and method for supporting social behavior. However, polyvagal theory differs from NMT and the window of tolerance model in useful ways. For example, while NMT also suggests a developmental chronology and associated neurological problems, polyvagal theory integrates the autonomic nervous system hierarchy into its model, focusing on the sense of safety that manifests within the nervous system. Similarly, while polyvagal theory posits that there are three states of physiologic response, which is analogous to the window of tolerance model, in polyvagal theory, the hierarchy is ordered according to a physiologic and structural understanding of the autonomic nervous system.

It is important to understand that while polyvagal theory has deeply impacted my work and consequently the framework that constitutes IAFT, it is a complicated subject with roots in neuroscience. Here, I offer the basics and explain how these inform IAFT.

Polyvagal theory is so useful to IAFT because it helps us understand and modulate an individual's physiologic responses to stimuli that signal danger and disconnection, or safety and connection. Its tool of detection is the vagus nerve. This large nerve travels between the brain and body—*vagus* is Latin for *wandering*—working on a sensate level to monitor external and internal stimuli and organize our reactions. The vagus nerve corresponds to and communicates with three "neurophysiological substrates" (Porges, 2009), retained in the autonomic nervous system as phylogenetically ordered subsystems: the dorsal vagal nerve, the sympathetic nervous system, and the ventral vagal nerve.

The lowest and most primitive subsystem is the dorsal vagus. This branch of the vagus nerve is connected to the organs underneath the diaphragm, like the stomach, intestines, liver, and kidneys. The dorsal branch is the most protective, least sensate, and least regulated. When it sends signals to the brain that are translated as extreme danger or fatal, the autonomic nervous system activates the dorsal vagal subsystem, initiating a profound disconnection that causes the individual to shut down, withdraw, go numb, play dead, or totally dissociate. When the dorsal branch is dominant, a person is least functional. In session, we may perceive the effects of dorsal dominance when a child appears to not listen, not engage, not participate in conversation, not use words, shrug their shoulders, or repeat, "I don't know." They may also seem apathetic, slow, checked out, remote, or removed.

The middle subsystem is the sympathetic nervous system, which is located above the dorsal vagus and connects to the heart and lungs. Whereas the dorsal vagal branch is associated with immobilization, the sympathetic branch is associated with mobilization. When the sympathetic nervous system detects danger, it initiates the body's built-in fight-or-flight response. This can manifest as an impulse to strike or hit, a clenched jaw, or a pounding heart. Like the dorsal vagal branch, when the sympathetic nervous system is activated, the individual does not feel safe, and they are not able to be open, connected, and relaxed in their environment and with the people around them. Instead, they seek confrontation or aggression. In session, we may perceive the effects of sympathetic nervous system dominance when a child appears to have chaotic energy, such as acting silly, running around, or displaying hyperactive behaviors like oppositionality or aggression.

The highest and evolutionarily newest subsystem is the ventral vagal nerve (Porges, 1995), which connects to our face, ears, eyes, throat, and heart. When the vagus nerve sends signals to the brain that are translated as signals of safety, the autonomic nervous system activates the ventral vagus, initiating a sense of connection and well-being. In polyvagal terms, the ventral subsystem is also known as the social engagement system (SES), because it manifests in our ability to connect with others through listening, eye contact, tone of voice, touch, and gestures.

When a person is in a ventral vagal mode, they feel that their environment is safe, that the people around them are friendly and well-intentioned and want the best for them. They also feel that their body is their ally, and they feel friendly toward it. (In contrast, a person in sympathetic vagal mode might feel an uncomfortable amount of energy, which can manifest in feeling unsettled, nervous, or fidgety. They might also feel pressure, tension, or pent-up anger. In dorsal vagal mode, a person might feel disconnected or cut off from their body and numb.) In session, we strive to foster a sense of ventral vagal safety in our clients. We may perceive the effects of ventral vagal dominance when the client appears to be open, interested, and cooperative through responsiveness, eye contact, voice modulation, and other capacities.

In polyvagal theory, the vagus nerve serves as the means of connection and the access point by which we can modulate the body's responses, affect, and correspondent behaviors. However, the vagus nerve does not operate according to a top-down or even bidirectional model; instead, it nonconsciously detects information on a cellular level, through a process known as *neuroception* (Porges, 2004), and sends it to the brain for neurological processing. It detects environmental, or external, information, such as air temperature, light, sounds, sensations, and people, as well as their associated signals of safety or threat. It also detects interoceptive, or internal, information, including pain or anxiety-provoking thoughts or memories.

The process by which the vagus nerve picks up nonconscious information and delivers it to the brain is important because, according to polyvagal theory, the brain's neurological processing typically uses this information to create a story or an explanatory narrative. Sometimes the nonconscious information is translated into a story that *things are good; we are safe*. At other times, it is translated into a story that *things are suspicious; we may not be safe*. This story can drive us to think certain things and behave in certain ways, regardless of outside objectivity. For the purposes of our work as IAFT therapists, this and other aspects of polyvagal theory offer both (1) a logical, accessible, and useful explanation for how and why people respond in suboptimal ways to stressful situations and (2) tools for healing the ability to connect and to strengthen existing connections. This makes it particularly useful when working with a parent-child dyad and their energetic interactions.

To bring this to life, let's consider how polyvagal theory can help us understand and respond to a common experience. Let's say I'm on the subway. Let's also say I ate a raspberry danish before boarding the subway, even though I promised myself I would no longer eat raspberry danishes because they make me feel sluggish and unhealthy. I'm on the subway platform deep underground, and the steel beams holding up the ceiling and platform seem rusty. I board the train, and I see a person with a menacing stare looking at me. The subway car wheels squeak. The train fuel fumes waft through the car. I begin to feel nauseous and trapped, but I'm not sure why. I glance at my phone and see a million emails I haven't responded to. One email catches my eye, and I start thinking about how late I am on completing work related to a committee of which I am a member. I then imagine the faces of the people in the committee—I see them going through all of my past mistakes on a ledger, and I see that they've decided to kick me out of the organization. I begin to feel persecuted and overwhelmed. I wonder how I'll be able to support myself when everyone finds out I'm a fraud.

For some readers, this illustrates a familiar train of thought. In fact, you might wonder, *Aren't these just cognitive distortions* (if you take a CBT point of view), or *a disapproving, critical father* (if you take a psychodynamic point of view), or *an insecurity based in previously uncontained negative affect that caused me to feel alone and ashamed* (if you take an attachment point of view)?

The answer is yes, all of the above. In addition, however, polyvagal theory suggests that physiologic aspects—the high blood sugar as a result of the danish, my sense of the threat of being buried underground, the menacing look of another passenger, the loud brake noise and fumes—all caused my body to feel unsafe. (These physiological aspects were undoubtedly evoked or inflamed by early memories and experiences in childhood, although this is not its emphasis.) Then, when I was reminded of the work I hadn't finished, my body, already in a panic, immediately went to thoughts of persecution and then oblivion. The determination that I am a no-good, rotten professional who will soon be in the gutter was a story made up by the sense-making, narrative-seeking part of my brain, and it was then attached to the panic in my body.

Through the lens of polyvagal theory, however, I can reorient my attention from the *story* to the various *stimuli* of which I may be unaware. My nervous system experienced sensations of a lack of safety, which is why my mind raced toward catastrophic thoughts. When I can attribute these thoughts to a physiologic response rather than to my faulty morality or rotten personality, I can feel a tremendous sense of compassion. It is not my fault that I became stuck in my story; rather, it is simply that my body did not feel safe. What do I need to do? I need to help my body feel better: I need air, I need to breathe, I need to talk myself through this train ride with some type of soothing mantra. As soon as I can get out of the subway, I need to move so as not to feel trapped. I need to rest after that, perhaps get a cup of tea and take a break or talk to a safe friend, so I can regain my equilibrium. Polyvagal theory offers me an explanation and an applicable set of tools for responding to feelings of discomfort or danger in this situation. To put this another way, its graspable map of the autonomic nervous system and the process it offers for activating the SES enables me to achieve equilibrium and thus find a sense of safety.

Applying Polyvagal Theory in Session

What can IAFT therapists do with this information in sessions with parents and children? A lot! From an IAFT therapist's view, a dysfunctional parent-child dyad is one in which one or both members feel unsafe and unconnected. The IAFT therapist therefore works with the child and parent's polyvagal responses to foster safety and connection. Once connection is established, the therapist harnesses the energy of the parent-child dyad to tone and ultimately strengthen their SES. This requires careful observation and assessment, as well as hands-on activities that help to stimulate both the child's and the parent's ventral responses and motivate their SES. Only when both clients are in ventral vagal mode can they strengthen and deepen their connection.

To do this work, we engage polyvagal theory in session through the following steps:

1. We observe and assess both the parent and the child in terms of their energetic responses, deciphering whether their physiologic responses are situated in the dorsal vagal, sympathetic, or ventral vagal branches, or a combination of branches.

2. We help the parent understand the autonomic nervous system and its impact on human behaviors on the most basic level, teaching them to gauge their own autonomic nervous system responses, to offer themselves compassion, and to uncover and identify what activities or people help activate their SES.

3. We teach the parent how to look at their child's behaviors from a polyvagal perspective rather than a moral perspective and guide them on how to provide SES-based interventions that lead to greater connectivity.

As IAFT therapists, we first gain the ability to engage the SES in clinic by observing and assessing our own polyvagal responses and by familiarizing ourselves with the fundamentals of the ventral vagal system. This includes mapping our own autonomic nervous system and understanding the various stimuli that correspond to our experiences of a dorsal vagal, sympathetic, and ventral vagal state. While our experiences can also include blended modes, I focus on the three primary modes. Mapping our autonomic nervous system is an incredibly useful tool for self-discovery and self-compassion, but its utility is also in the practice it offers for better understanding and helping to manage our clients' energetic responses.

Mapping the Autonomic Ladder

The concept of mapping the autonomic nervous system comes from Deb Dana's (2018, 2020a, 2020b) work on the polyvagal "ladder," which gives us insight into what circumstances, conditions, events, or people provoke feelings of comfort and safety, and what circumstances, conditions, events, or people make us feel unsafe, uncertain, nervous, anxious, or shut down. In the ladder exercise, we conceptualize the autonomic nervous system as a ladder with various rungs representing the different vagal modes. The ladder begins with our nervous system—it proceeds from the bottom up rather than from the top down, which enables us to more objectively examine our physiologic reactions to internal and external cues that contribute to our understanding of ourselves and the world.

To complete the ladder exercise, use the diagram on the next page and a writing utensil. Take a moment to familiarize yourself with the diagram, then proceed through the instructions that follow.

You're going to take a walk in your imagination, and your journey will begin with the dorsal vagal branch. Close your eyes (or not, depending on your comfort level) and find a comfortable position. Now think of people, instances, places, or memories that made you or make you feel frozen. This might be a robotic feeling, in which you feel like you are going through the motions but are not actually there. Or it may feel like you are on the outside looking in. For some people, being in a dorsal vagal state may involve a feeling of wanting to hide or a feeling of *I can't deal with this*. You may also feel like you just don't care about what's going on outside and feel checked out. Jot down some notes about these experiences in the space in the center column and bottom row of the diagram.

To the left of these notes, on the dorsal rungs of the ladder, write down a few words that represent what caused you to feel this way. You might, for

The Autonomic Ladder*

Autonomic Ladder	Thoughts, Incidents, Memories, Time Periods, Places	How I Reacted/Behaved
Ventral		
Sympathetic		
Dorsal		

* Adapted from *Polyvagal Flip Chart*, by D. Dana, 2020, Norton Professional Books.

instance, remember when you got a blank stare from your son when you were enthusiastically asking him about his day at school. From this memory, you might extract the words *rejected* and *sickened* and write them on the dorsal rungs.

Now turn to the sympathetic nervous system. Try to recall people, instances, places, or memories that caused you to feel a sense of being reactive or fired up. Maybe you were doing something that required some urgency, or maybe it was a stressful day or period in your life when you had to manage a lot of things. Maybe there was a crisis or emergency where you had to respond at a rapid-fire rate. You might, for example, remember when a loved one had an injury. You might have a stressful, chaotic household or job and feel like you are constantly putting out fires. Maybe you remember a dangerous experience, such as a literal fire, from which you had to evacuate. Record your notes in the center column, then write down some words on sympathetic rungs that represent these memories.

Last, focus on the top rungs, the ventral vagal branch. Think of people, instances, places, or memories that caused you to feel completely at home and comfortable, completely accepted and connected. You may feel joyful and energetic, or you may feel relaxed and calm. Regardless, the sense you're striving to identify is one of feeling accepted the way you are. Think of those memories and write down your notes in the center, then some representative words on the sympathetic rungs on your ladder.

Visual Analysis

Now that you've labeled your ladder, take your diagram and hold it at arm's length. Don't read the words; just focus on the visual elements. How many examples did you write down for each rung? How much ink did you expend on each example? How forceful is the writing? Is the handwriting different? Where are there fewer descriptions? Where are there more?

The varying quality or volume of the writing may simply reflect how much you felt the incidents in your body and how they translated to your fine motor skills through your hand and onto the paper. If you wrote more descriptions in the sympathetic nervous system section and fewer in the dorsal vagal section, it may mean that you are often operating from that place in your autonomic nervous system. Or it might mean that the dorsal vagal memories are too overwhelming to consider in the context of this exercise. In visually analyzing your autonomic ladder, you do not judge; instead, you gather information and become more familiar with stimuli and their correspondences to your autonomic nervous system and to your narratives.

Reflection on Response

To provoke further reflection on your autonomic ladder, ask yourself how you behaved and responded to particular incidents, writing down your answers in the column to the right. For example, if, in the dorsal vagal area, you wrote that your son gave you a blank stare when you asked him about his day, and you felt rejected and frozen, you will want to explain what you did next. You may have slumped your shoulders and turned away from your son. You may have gotten quiet and felt disengaged. You may have rummaged through the pantry and eaten a sweet snack as a way of soothing yourself. Again, the point is not to judge, but to observe and reflect.

Purpose of the Exercise

This exercise helps to shed light on the connection between the autonomic nervous system and our behavior as it relates to ourselves and others. On a very basic level, it helps make clear that the responses we have to others are informed by the autonomic nervous system's effort to keep us safe. When the vagus nerve detects stimuli, the autonomic nervous system responds with a signal. If it could talk, it might say something like *I don't feel safe, and I'm trying to protect myself.* The safety response can take the form of discharging excess or unwanted energy from the body by shutting it out or by expelling it.

This is useful information for anyone. However, it is especially useful when working with parents who are permissive, detached, or passive; with parents who fight with their child, yell at them, or fly off the handle in a rage; or with parents who fluctuate between passivity and resentment. All of these are autonomic nervous system responses working, on a very primitive level, to keep the parent safe. This information also helps us understand our clients' narrativization tendency as an effort to rationalize and make sense of these automatic, nonconscious responses. While this might seem simple and intuitive, in the context of the therapeutic paradigm, it helpfully relocates the locus of guilt, blame, and shame that is so troublesome for so many clients.

This exercise allows one to begin to more actively manage one's own autonomic nervous system—which is helpful for clients and clinicians alike. First, it helps us to identify what physiological responses we associate with a ventral vagal mode and to prioritize the actions that will allow us to spend more time there. For instance, perhaps after mapping your nervous system, you see that you often feel calm and in a state of comfortable flow when you are the first in your household to wake up in the morning and enjoy a warm cup of tea, silently contemplating the view out the window. Recognizing this, you might then prioritize that experience, maybe even deepening it with reflection or meditation. You might also begin to call forth the feeling associated with this experience when you feel threatened or otherwise in a sympathetic nervous system or dorsal vagal state.

Second, the polyvagal ladder helps us see when we are not in a ventral vagal state, which can then help us recognize opportunities to practice self-compassion when we need it most. For example, perhaps you see that you feel panicked when dealing with a particular situation at work. Recognizing this, you are better equipped to notice the signs of this panic—shortness of breath, increased heart rate, a flushed face—the next time they occur and recognize them as your nervous system reacting to stimuli, not as an indication that you are too weak to handle pressure. You can then take steps to moderate your nervous system's response by slowing and deepening your breath and cooling your face.

To really bring home how mapping your nervous system can help you more actively manage your ANS, I want to share my own experience. Although I'm typically rather moderate in my reactions, sometimes I have surges of energy where I feel quite belligerent, such as when I'm feeling very stressed or when I've slept poorly the previous night. During those times, my reactions aren't always moderate. I might be driving, for instance, and when somebody starts to tail me and then tries to pass me, I might feel a flash of anger and find myself thinking something like *Oh no, you won't*. Sometimes, I even rev my engine, switch lanes, speed up, and make a move to block the other driver. This is obviously a problem, and most of us would probably call it road rage.

However, when I can catch myself after that first surge of sympathetic nervous system energy—that flash of anger—and take a deep breath and say to myself, *Dafna, you're in a sympathetic nervous system state: your nervous system is not feeling safe, and you're experiencing some type of danger*, I can then calm down. I can imagine, for instance, a loving parent rocking me to soothe me, or a blanket made of fibers of love from the loving people in my life, wrapping around my body.

Mapping the autonomic ladder is a tool for this kind of self-compassion and management. When you're better able to manage your own ANS, you're also better able to listen and respond to your clients and to help them manage themselves.

The Social Engagement System

The SES is both an expression of our vagal state and a way of regulating it (as well as that of the other person with whom we are relating; Porges, 2018). In fact, we can think of the SES as something that is turned on or off by polyvagal modes. When we are in a dorsal vagal mode, our SES is turned off, and we are typically unable to connect with ourselves or with others. When we are in a ventral vagal mode, our SES is turned on, and we are usually capable of making strong connections. When the SES is on, it communicates, through nonconscious mechanisms, that we are safe to connect with others and that others are safe to connect with us. As with mapping our autonomic ladder, by familiarizing ourselves with the fundamentals of the SES and by practicing activities that strengthen this familiarity, we become more capable of staying in a ventral vagal state and using our SES to connect with ourselves and our clients.

You can imagine the SES in action by thinking of someone in your life who seems to have a magic touch when it comes to relating to others. Most of us know someone like this—someone who has a way of calming a tense situation or putting people at ease, someone who can quickly connect with strangers on the bus or while waiting in line. These are typically people who are operating in a ventral vagal mode with a strong SES. When the ventral vagus is dominant, it activates social engagement circuitry that then regulates the types of vocalizations, facial expressions, and gestures that elicit feelings of trust and openness in another person. Our facial expressions, tone of voice, and head gestures nonconsciously signal to another person, *I have good intentions and am interested in cooperating with you.*

Let's take a look at the primary elements of the SES and the subtle ways emotional messages of safety and openness to connection are transmitted.

Voice Prosody

Prosody refers to the emotional meaning beyond the words in a conversation. Prosody includes the timing, phrasing, emphasis, and intonation that help convey aspects of meaning and make our speech lively, convincing, and engaging. It's conveyed by the raising and lowering of pitch, the speeding up or slowing of rhythm, and the loudness of the words spoken. Even the frequency of breathing within speech can convey a sense of urgency or calmness through the length of the phrases and pauses. In conversation, your effective use of prosody can create a sense that you're really following and getting what your conversational partner is saying. When you're talking, it's also the feature of storytelling that keeps the listener interested and curious. Using a prosodic voice captures and holds the attention of the listener, thereby organizing and calming their nervous system.

The most elemental model of producing prosody comes from the sounds a parent makes while talking to a 4- or 5-month-old baby. For example, imagine that Josh is chatting with his baby daughter, Bella, while dressing her on the changing table:

JOSH [*pulling Bella's arm out of the pajama shirt*]: Where's Bella's arm? Ooooh, there it is! What a big girl you are. You're getting so biiigggg.

BELLA: Ba!

JOSH [*in a high-pitched, excited tone*]: That's right! Big! Who's a big girl?

BELLA [*making a gurgling, babbling noise with her lips*]: Brrrrrrrrrrrr.

JOSH [*putting the clean shirt over Bella's head, speaking with increasing volume and inflection in his voice*]: Where'd you go? Where'd you go, Bella? [*Pulls shirt to discover Bella's eyes.*] Boo!

BELLA: [*Looks momentarily startled, then smiles wide, wiggling her whole body and squealing as she giggles.*]

JOSH: You're so silly. You're so silly. I got your tummy! [*Leans down to blow raspberries on her belly.*] I got your belly!

BELLA: [*Kicks her legs and lets out another, louder squeal.*]

JOSH: You're so funny, aren't ya, little girl?

Later, when they're in the kitchen, Josh uses the coffee grinder, and Bella is startled by the growling, loud noise. She gasps in shock and then lets out a shrill cry.

JOSH [*speaking with quick, urgent breaths*]: Oh! Oh, Bella! Come here. [*Picks her up from the high chair.*] Oh, that startled you, didn't it? 'Cause you didn't know what that was. [*Shifts to speaking in a soft, cooing, slow voice as he rocks her.*] You were looking at your banana and then Daddy made that loud 'grrr' noise from the coffee grinder and you didn't know what that was. I'm sorry, baby. It's okay.

BELLA: [*Quickly shifts from a scream to a whimper and then sighs as she settles her head on her father's shoulder.*]

This parent-infant dialogue is the essential foundation for prosody in human beings (Bowlby, 1983; Stern, 2018; Trevarthen & Aitken, 2001). Humans use a particular voice instinctively while tending to babies because babies are biologically programmed to respond to higher-pitched notes that lilt up and down, like the chirping of a flock of lively birds on a spring morning. This type of voice captures babies' attention and make them calmer, more organized, and more amenable to the parents' suggestions and handling. Conversely, babies aren't as naturally able to interpret lower-pitched, grumbly noises, which tend to signal danger (like a lion's roar) or monotonous sounds, usually lower in pitch, which seem controlled and unemotional.

A prosodic voice is an essential component—not only for a parent but also for a therapist—by which to convey empathy. The true masters of prosody really stand out when you watch them in action. Daniel A. Hughes, the creator of dyadic developmental psychotherapy (DDP)—about which I have much more to say in the next chapter—is one such person. His captivating use of that singsongy voice while matching the rhythm of his client is like witnessing the unfolding of a whole concert of flow and meaning-making. In a conversation on video that I've watched many times, Hughes (2009) is sitting face-to-face with a mother who's experiencing almost categorical rejection from her 12-year-old adopted daughter. The mother, out of her own underlying feelings of hopelessness and hurt, was actively hostile to Hughes earlier in the session. After a long back-and-forth with Hughes, in which the mother struggles to uncover her true pain, she finally begins to trust Hughes's intentions and reveal her deep suffering.

CLIENT [*leaning forward, face contorted in pain, gasping in short breaths and heaving as she speaks*]: I let this child into my heart.

HUGHES [*in a pained, high-pitched yet encouraging whisper and gasp*]: Yeah.

CLIENT: I offered her everything a child could want! A loving home, a mother who's interested in her—who wants to know what she feels, what her day was like!

HUGHES [*sitting forward, matching her expression of pain*]: Yeah.

CLIENT: I want to help her—with anything! Anything at all! But she won't let me! I would've given anything for my mom to want me like that!

HUGHES [*takes a deep breath and speaks with urgency, matching the client's cadence*]: Of course you would! [*Repeating more softly.*] Of course you would. You brought her in. You cared for her. You thought of everything you could to make her feel comfortable, to make her feel safe, to make her feel wanted. [*Pauses, sighs, and speaks in a quieter, slower voice.*] You're saying, "Hey, I'm your mom."

CLIENT [*pauses her crying, looks intently at him, and sighs deeply*]: Yeah.

When I close my eyes and listen to this segment without the video, I can almost imagine Hughes holding the mother, rocking her back and forth as she's experiencing her excruciating sense of rejection. His pitch, rhythm, and cadence conveyed both empathy and comfort, and made the mother calmer and more receptive to letting him in. It seems almost magical.

Resonance

Another component of the SES that fosters connection by eliciting trust is the use of a resonant voice. *Resonance* refers to your ability to use the body to vibrate in sympathy with the sound of your voice. In the therapist's room, it's the classic response of the therapist's convincing *mm-hmm*. It comes when you open up your lungs (by breathing deeply), open up your throat (by yawning), and relax your jaw. In fact, the more relaxed you are and the more space you create in your body cavity, the more resonance you can produce. Resonance makes the person with whom you're speaking feel convinced that you understand the intensity of their feeling. It helps show that two people are vibrating in the same frequency. It suggests, *I understand you.* Some people have a naturally resonant voice—think of the actor Morgan Freeman or singers Janis Joplin and Louis Armstrong. When we listen to these performers, we feel wholly convinced of the emotions they're transmitting, and we're carried away by their message.

Imagine, for example, an angry teenager who's been given the ultimatum of going to therapy or having his phone taken away indefinitely. He's resentful, hostile, and defensive as he sits on your couch. He stares sullenly at the wall, and when you ask him what's going on, he lets out a tirade: "I don't know why I have to come to this stupid place every week! I only came because my mom told me she'd take my phone. I know you're the one who told her to do that!" An outburst like this can cause even the most experienced therapist to momentarily retreat inward in defense. But this reaction will constrict your throat and lungs, and you'll produce a thinner, more monotonous vocal tone, which may contribute to the client getting more upset. Why? Because he senses your retreat, and his worst fear—that he's no good and rotten—is confirmed.

When you motivate your SES instead—pausing to sit up, setting your shoulders back, taking a deep belly breath, and opening your throat before speaking—you will produce a more convincing sound while responding, "Ohhh, okay. Thank you for telling me that. Now I understand part of the reason why you came in here in such a crummy mood." This young man wants you to *really understand*, to *really feel* his internal sense of pain and fear of rejection. The vibration behind your words, more than the words themselves, will help convince him that you do.

Take a moment, as an exercise, to put your fingers on your lips, take a deep breath, yawn in the back of your throat (while keeping your lips shut), and then let out a convincing *mm-hmm*. The more you can feel your lips vibrating, the more resonance you're achieving. Of course, you have to find just the right measure of resonance when you communicate or you may sound overly passionate or intrusive. But it's usually the underuse of resonance rather than overuse that leads to miscommunication.

Facial Expressions

The SES also guides our use of facial expressions to elicit trust. Porges hypothesizes that there's a "face-heart connection" in the body (Porges, 2018, p. 57), wherein the movements of the facial muscles regulate or change a person's heart rate, serving to create either relaxation and openness or defensiveness and guardedness. The facial expressions that evoke positive social states include having a genuine smile; a focused, curious look in your eyes; and a wide, smooth (unfurrowed) brow and forehead.

What do these facial states look like? Have a friend take a photo of your face while you conjure up different images of feeling states, such as a baby smiling at you, a reunion with a cherished friend, a moment when you received distressing news, or a time when you felt confused by some information that didn't make sense to you. Then take a close look at your faces in these different feeling states. Let yourself imagine which expressions you might use to create feelings of trust, and which might interfere with connecting with a client.

Now let's take a closer look at a genuine smile (as opposed to a "say *cheese*" smile) and its utility with clients. In a genuine smile, the eyes close a bit as the muscles around the eyes tense, wrinkles appear on the sides of the eyes because the face muscles pull the cheeks up and make them bigger, and the skin under the lower lip tightens so the bottom teeth are covered up. In other words, the person is smiling with their eyes. It's difficult at first, but not impossible, to evoke a genuine smile in a situation that doesn't normally inspire one, such as meeting a client who brings up a feeling of discomfort or dread for you.

Although you may worry that needing to use these facial gymnastics to produce a smile means you are not being authentic, remember that a client who is rejecting or intimidating is likely defending against a fear that you will judge or scorn them. By evoking a warm smile upon greeting them, you nonconsciously affect their brain, signaling a message for connection: *Give it a chance; it could turn out all right.* In effect, you're overriding their own internal message and helping them choose a noncongruent response. You're saying, *Yes, I know you're fearful, but I'm still open to you.*

Another powerful message of safety and connection is signaled through your eyebrows and forehead, which play an important role in indicating true acceptance and curiosity about another person's negative feeling states. Often, when clients express feelings of defensiveness or aggression, our immediate reaction of a furrowed brow provides a nonconscious message back to them that we've internalized their negative messages and believe in their inner badness. It's hard not to have this response if a depressed client is talking monotonously about the worthlessness of the world, or if an anxious client spends countless minutes expressing obsessive thoughts and out-of-control feelings. Even if a client is sharing something profound and you're grappling with it, your eyes might naturally close a little and one of your eyebrows will droop, or the two lines between your eyebrows will form a *V* shape. Your intent is to convey deep thought, but a client whose brain has been overtrained to detect judgment and scorn may read this pensive or concerned look as condemnation. Managing the muscles around your eyes, ears, and forehead can help correct that effect, enabling you to send your preferred message: *I'm truly open and curious about you.*

To motivate your SES and connect through facial expressions, elevate your eyebrows so that your eyelids are taut and not drooping. This look is subtly different from just looking surprised. To help train yourself, look in the mirror and raise your eyebrows up and down. While doing this, focus on moving your eyebrows out toward your ears. If you want to perfect this expression, you can work on the art of wiggling your ears. This is a capacity that some people have innately, some can learn, and some can't do at all for physiologic reasons. But attempting to learn this trick (and others, like flaring your nostrils or darting one eyebrow at a time) will increase your overall control of your facial muscles so you can consciously create a more open, smooth brow line and forehead to signal receptivity rather than suspicion or judgment.

Gestures and Posture

Another key illustrator of safety and connection is the use of gestures, both of the head and hands, as well as your overall posture. We are reassured when a speaker's body language is congruent with their speech. For example, slumping, slouching, or tilting one's head down signals lack of energy or interest, a closed-off look, or possibly anger. To make use of the relationship between the SES and gestures and posture, you can be mindful about sitting back in your chair, relaxing your shoulders back and down, sitting up straight, and taking a nice, deep breath from the belly. Tilting your chin up a degree or two and angling your neck out slightly can also communicate a sense of openness and vulnerability. Leaning forward is a sign of intense interest and can be mindfully used to show focus and investment in the client's story or to emphasize a crucial point you wish to convey.

The degree to which hand gestures are used to convey or emphasize a point in a story varies from culture to culture. However, using gestures to illustrate a point in a story can set the listener's brain at ease because it helps make your message congruent and clear. For clients who lack basic trust, any sign of ambiguity or lack of congruence between your body language and words will register as suspicion of your motive. So, while most of us were taught (mostly through modeling) that our hands should be calm and static on our laps while we engage with our clients, strategic use of posture and gestures can, in fact, enhance a sense of safety by highlighting our intention to engage and connect throughout our bodies.

Eye Contact and Touch

As listeners, we tend to look in a sustained way at a speaker to show our interest and attention. But beyond that, what in a person's eyes lets us know they're really listening? What produces bright eyes rather than a dull look? The SES indicates that one answer can be found in the difference between the meaning of the two words *looking* and *gazing*. *Looking* simply refers to the act of directing your eyes in a particular direction. *Gazing* refers to the act of looking at something in a steady way, usually for a longer time period, and possibly with less blinking. The difference is difficult to explain but easy to distinguish if you're the object of a listener's gaze.

The pupils in the eyes of a listener who's really engaged will dilate. Although this difference is subtle enough that we don't usually perceive it with the naked eye, the brain registers this as a signal of genuine interest. Personally, I practice showing this interest by focusing on one of my client's eyes at a time, trying to notice the varying colors in the iris. I've noticed that when you really look at the eye, it's fascinating how variegated and broad the spectrum of colors can be. For me, this brings a palpable feeling of humanity toward whomever I'm sitting with. As I look, I imagine that right behind that person's eyes is their soul or spirit, and that gives fuller meaning to my gaze. This is a useful illustration for the perpetuating power of the SES. When we work with the SES to communicate and solicit connection with others, we are easier to connect with in turn, which then makes us more likely to connect.

The therapeutic use of touch is another powerful signal of safety when applied in an attuned way. Touch between therapists and adult clients is usually discouraged, but there's a strong argument to be made for incorporating calming or reassuring touch when warranted. With the client's permission and with awareness of their physiologic responses, you might offer to gently press a client's hand or to place a hand on their shoulder. When direct contact isn't appropriate, even approximating warm touch can be effective. For example, preparing a warm mug of tea for a client to grasp on a cold day, having plush throw blankets of various textures available for the client to hold or drape around their shoulders, or supplying various weight pillows for them to clutch can provide tremendous comfort to calm and contain feelings of vulnerability.

I also try to establish the practice of shaking my client's hand before they leave. I do this with intention, trying to avoid a "let's close this meeting" effect and instead grasping with both hands and looking warmly into their eyes to solidify a sense of *let's have this one last moment of connection to solidify the gains we've made.* It also signifies *I'll hold you in my mind until the next time we meet.* I don't do this with every client or at every session, but I often try it if I sense that a consolidating touch will help the client walk out the door feeling more grounded.

The Social Engagement System in Action

Polyvagal theory has uncovered physiological mechanics of connection that enable us to respond to and modulate connection with clients in session. Additionally, when a session goes off-course, we can understand more precisely the nature of the disconnection and how to repair it on a very basic, somatic level. The more we are able to identify the "What just happened?" moments, the more we can, in a systematic way, regain connection with the client. This is the essence of what IAFT is all about.

One such moment occurred in a session with 15-year-old Beth and her mom, Maria. Right from the start, Maria looked tense; she told me that her daughter had a tantrum in the car because they didn't have time to go to the drugstore to get the lip gloss that Beth wanted. This was a pattern between the dyad—some ostensibly small disappointment set off an explosion between them that resulted in days of hurt feelings and distance. Beth walked in and paced my office as if lost. I sensed that some type of physical experience would help organize her, so I offered a simple game of throw and catch to the rhythm of a song. But as soon as I said it, Beth slumped onto the couch and retorted, "No!" Maria rolled her eyes in exasperation. Beth drew the hood of her coat over her eyes. Her shoulders were slumped, her eyes were hidden, and her mouth angled downward in a frown. Maria started cajoling her daughter to cooperate, but I sensed that trying to confront Beth would only cause her to retreat further.

"Wait, wait, Mom!" I said breathlessly, conveying a sense of urgency. "Maybe, just maybe, what's going on here is that Beth is trying to cooperate but she's feeling so intensely about things right now that she just can't look at us. It's too much. *Too much,*" I said pleadingly. I wanted my tone of voice to let Beth know, *I get you, girl—this is serious. You were in no mood to play. You're hurt.* I kept talking in a singsongy voice, directing my words toward Maria but speaking in a way that resonated with Beth's sense of feeling rattled by getting out of control. My words flowed like a calming story but with strong forward momentum. I expressed what I thought had happened before she got upset and wondered about what it must have been like to feel that way. That singsongy, resonant voice allowed both mom and daughter to calm a bit.

Slowly, Beth raised her hood from her eyes until she was looking at me. I returned her gaze and held my hands out to my sides in a question stance. "Was any of that close to what you experienced?" I said this with curiosity and without being wedded to any particular answer. Beth nodded in agreement. Getting the eye contact and the back-and-forth communication flowing was my goal. Beth was now open to the possibility that her mom and I wanted to be with her and to share her experience. That shared moment helped the rest of the session move toward a place of greater understanding between Beth and Maria.

The discovery and use of the SES—and the corollary knowledge of the ways that prosodic voice, eye contact, gestures, and gentle touch affect social communication—represent a significant advancement in the field of psycho-therapy and brain science. By being aware of these different modes of communication, we can understand what happens when we lose the connection with our client and know where to go to find it again. Ultimately, polyvagal theory, and the SES in particular, helps to structure and support the energetic work that, in IAFT, is the medium for communicating safety and establishing and strengthening connection in the therapy room. By enabling us to approach safety and connection from a neurological perspective, polyvagal theory offers access to all other growth.

3

Theraplay, Dyadic Developmental Psychotherapy, and the Autobiographical Narrative

While polyvagal theory provides important theoretical and operational context for IAFT, in this chapter, I turn to two other critical inputs that inform the IAFT therapist's work: Theraplay and dyadic developmental psychotherapy (DDP). Both of these approaches are trademarked therapies that require extensive training for certification. As I described earlier, IAFT combines exercises and activities from both, adding more explicit instructions on how to connect the two. This, in effect, helps to expand the utility of both models. All three therapeutic approaches are allied by a joint focus on attachment and the parent-child dyad, wherein the dyad is viewed as the mechanism by which attachment security, resiliency, and a sense of self are strengthened.

In IAFT, strengthening attachment through connection happens at three different, interconnected stages: (1) the therapist works to connect with the parent, (2) the therapist works to connect with the child, and (3) the therapist teaches the parent to connect with the child and works to facilitate the parent-child connection. Attunement, co-regulation, and intersubjectivity are the means through which these points of connection are strengthened. Theraplay and DDP offer a variety of tools for enhancing these capacities.

Theraplay

Theraplay is particularly meaningful to me for the reasons I described in the introduction. In fact, because I'm a certified Theraplay practitioner, I know just how effective Theraplay can be for healing children's attachment issues. Theraplay essentially puts polyvagal theory to work, offering parents the opportunity to connect with their child through play, but in more intimate, foundational ways. In Theraplay sessions, which are videotaped, we guide the parent and child through a series of interactive, playful, face-to-face activities. Although these activities are fun, fun is not the goal. Rather, the activities help the parent learn to lend their *whole self* to their child. This, in turn, helps the child modulate and organize their experiences with and expectations of trusted others. Through repeated, predictable patterns of play, a child learns, perhaps for the first time, to interact with their parent in a trusting way. This helps activate and strengthen the connection between parent and child.

Because Theraplay allows children to reset their nonconscious expectations of what happens when they interact with others, it is undertaken with the goal of changing the child's implicit relational knowing. Many of the children with whom Theraplay practitioners work have insecure attachment patterns. For these children, maybe because of a parent's weak attunement, or maybe because of a parent's inability or unwillingness to co-regulate, the child's implicit relational knowing assumes their parent is not a source of safety and connection. Theraplay-informed techniques create interpersonal experiences that are noncongruent with a child's insecure internal working model. This challenges their brain to develop new, healthier implicit relational knowledge of what it is like to be in a relationship with their caregiver. The child therefore begins to learn what it is like to be in connected relationships more generally.

For a child who is described by their parent as defiant and uncooperative, Theraplay can challenge the child's—and the parent's—relational knowledge. I provided an illustration of this in chapter 1, when I described the game I played with Natasha in which we tested her strong arms. Now let's consider another example: Imagine you are in session with a little boy who is frustrated and struggling. He pushes you away with his legs. Rather than tell him, "No, we don't use our legs like that in here," you might instead take his legs in your hands and say, "Boy, you've got strong legs! Wow! You've got really strong legs! I bet you can't push me over with these legs on the count of three!" You might hold the child's two feet in the palms of your hands, count to three, and then, when the child pushes again, rock backward with a big "Ooohhh!" sound. When you come back up, you will likely see that the boy's face has changed from defensive fear to proud delight.

What just happened here? In this case, you were *attuned* to the child's bodily tension, offered a cooperative way of *co-regulating* the tension by creating a game of push-me-over, and then rolled out of it to show the child that you were delighted by his antics. This creates an *intersubjective* moment for the child. Games like these, the hallmark of Theraplay, help to reframe and organize a child's resistance into a moment of reciprocal play, giving the child an opportunity to experience themselves as strong, clever, and—most importantly—*connected* to a supportive adult, rather than as bad, rejected, and isolated from a supportive adult. In this way, a Theraplay practitioner can give a child new meaning for what it means to be themselves in the context of a safe and pleasurable relationship.

Theraplay is an excellent tool for strengthening the parent-child connection, and for interested practitioners, its certification process can be incredibly rewarding. However, IAFT differs from Theraplay in some ways. Primarily, IAFT prioritizes responsive flexibility within sessions and parent-specific session work. *Responsive flexibility* means that IAFT therapists do not privilege rigorously structured sessions with mandatory activities. Instead, IAFT therapists respond to negative reactions and feelings that arise during play activities with expressive curiosity, working to explore and discuss these feelings in the moment, sometimes at length. They then integrate variations on play activities that help to address the negative feeling.

For example, let's say a child, Alvin, and his dad are playing a beanbag-drop activity. They sit face-to-face, each with a beanbag on his head, dropping the beanbags into each other's hands at an agreed-upon cue word. Alvin repeatedly runs away from his dad while playing the activity, seemingly angry. A Theraplay practitioner might respond with an activity that brings Alvin back close: they may stand up, take Alvin's hands, and say, "Oh, look, you can balance the beanbag on your head while standing! Let's see if you can walk really slowly with it on your head back to where Dad is sitting." An IAFT therapist will also try a playful way to redirect the child. However, if Alvin continues to move away and pout, the IAFT therapist will use their knowledge of the SES and get demonstrably curious. They might modulate their tone of voice and say, "Hey, it's really okay if you don't like what's happening right now." Then they will use facial expressions or gestures of curiosity to wonder aloud about possibilities for interpreting Alvin's behavior: "I wonder what is going on for Alvin that makes him run away and feel so unhappy or yucky when Dad and I try to play the beanbag-drop game?"

By getting expressively, demonstrably curious, the IAFT therapist articulates for Alvin his fears, worries, or negative feelings based on their previous knowledge of his history and current relational problems with his parents. Perhaps Alvin feels worried that he will mess up and not catch the beanbag, and maybe that brings up feelings of not being good enough or fears of being rejected. Or maybe Alvin feels that the therapist and his dad set the activity's rules without listening to his thoughts or wishes. By wondering aloud about these possibilities, the IAFT therapist offers Alvin an opportunity to react, as well as an opportunity to be accepted and empathized with. This helps Alvin become more aware of his feelings and how he responds to situations when he feels rejected or unheard. Whereas in Theraplay, the set, structured activities prioritize safety and organize the play interactions, IAFT gives equal value to making meaning of the child's opposition or negative behaviors, using the common challenges of client sessions as opportunities to make conscious the meaning of the event in the context of the child's life.

IAFT also prioritizes parent work through psychoeducation and parent-only sessions. In fact, in IAFT, the parent is presented with a model for their own change. In other words, when parents come in, they are introduced to the framework, phases, and composition of the therapy. This includes understanding that the first part of the work will focus mostly on them. It also includes understanding that they will be taught about their nervous system responses and will be asked to practice using the PACE attitude (which we will explore in a few paragraphs) at home. They will also be asked about their own childhood experiences and be asked to reflect on how these experiences might affect their day-to-day parenting. They will be introduced to parent-only sessions as part of the work, including a phase of work that consists of consecutive parent-only sessions, during which the parent and therapist dive deeper into some of the more difficult issues that often arise.

Dyadic Developmental Psychotherapy

In addition to using modified elements of Theraplay, IAFT modifies elements of DDP, which Daniel A. Hughes developed after growing frustrated in his work with foster and adopted children. From Hughes's perspective, the clinical tools of the day were too focused on working on the child and teaching them skills for self-regulation. These tools were woefully insufficient for treating the very serious emotional and mental problems of abused and neglected children. Hughes therefore developed DDP to address children's need to understand their traumas in the crucible of a loving relationship with an attachment figure, using methods that did not rely on cognitive approaches or the child's ability to verbalize their feelings. DDP also helps parents become more aware of how their attachment histories affect their child and how to actively become agents of healing in their child's life.

DDP rests on a philosophical foundation of attachment that assumes a child cannot grow into a healthy adult without an organized sense of self developed in relationship to a caregiver. DDP consequently offers tools to support children who have a diffuse and disorganized sense of self due to weak attachment bonds. Its tools are designed to engage the child in a process of discovering, in the context of a loving, supportive other (ideally the primary caregiver, but often the therapist), their true, authentic thoughts, wishes, perceptions, feelings, and opinions about themselves and the world. Ultimately, one of the goals in DDP, as in IAFT and other attachment-based therapies, is to facilitate the child's safe and secure attachment to a loving, supportive other through which the child feels able to talk about hard things and know they will be accepted. Through the establishment of this secure base, the child gains the ability to know, trust, and accept themselves.

IAFT makes use of two important DDP tools—the PACE attitude and affective reflective (AR) dialogue—which are typically used to help the parent-child dyad co-create meaning. Generally speaking, co-created meaning is the result of a process whereby a person with an inchoate and unnamed thought or feeling is able, in the presence of and with the encouragement of another person, to become more aware of and to articulate that thought or feeling. It follows from the supportive presence of a compassionate, attuned listener who helps, often by their simple presence, a person to feel clearer and more settled about what they feel or think in a particular instance.

In the context of DDP, co-created meaning follows from the dyad's mutual understanding that a child must be able to speak to their parent about their wishes, beliefs, thoughts, and motives, and that their parent must be able to respond in supportive, empathic ways (rather than in judgmental or controlling ways). Co-created meaning might be the result of the parent's attunement. It might also be a consequence of the therapist's exaggerated reflection of the child's affect. In fact, by reflecting and intensifying the child's affect so as to make it conscious to the child, the therapist uses the tools of DDP to help the child begin to connect to these feelings. The connection validates these feelings, promoting the child's relief and release that often follows the sense of feeling understood and accepted.

PACE

As I mentioned in chapter 1, PACE is an acronym that reminds us to respond to a child's statements or behaviors—especially those that are challenging, negative, noncongruous, or irritating—with playfulness, acceptance, curiosity, and empathy. The PACE attitude is the ideal attitude held by the child's parent or caregiver, or a meaningful other. In the context of IAFT, as well as DDP, the sequence of the PACE attitude is usually (though not always) expressed first through acceptance, then through empathy, then through curiosity. Play is sprinkled throughout wherever possible, either as needed or when spontaneously inspired.

When a child makes a negative statement, an IAFT therapist first reacts with total, authentic acceptance. For instance, if a child says, "I should be allowed to play video games after school instead of doing homework because homework is boring," we don't show shock, dismay, or displeasure. In fact, we don't even show neutrality. We enthusiastically acknowledge their statement. By expressing a full-throated acceptance of their darker sentiment, we show the child that we understand and embrace this side of them, and are not offended, startled, hurt, or enraged.

Initial and immediate acceptance is important because when a child makes a statement that is challenging, provocative, upsetting, or uncomfortable, they are expressing one side of their internal dilemma. The child's dilemma is the same dilemma we all share: We often have mixed feelings about what we *want* to do and what we know we *should* do. Or we feel like we have two selves: a self that is cooperative and wants to please and a self that is angry and wants to dominate, go its own way, or act selfishly. By expressing this negative side, the child is taking a bold step in exposing their full sentiments. They are also putting us to the test. Will we react with rejection, disgust, or disdain? Will we regard them as foolish, immature, or stupid? We pass this test when we respond to the child's negativity with enthusiastic acceptance, saying something like "Hey, I'm glad to know what's on your mind" or "I gotcha, thanks for letting me know about that."

Next, with the PACE attitude in mind, we work to respond to the child with an empathic statement. This is not the kind of empathy that can be expressed in a dry clinical way, as in, "It sounds like you get mad when your mom tells you to do homework before playing video games." As IAFT therapists, we instead make use of the SES, putting our whole self into demonstrating that we really feel, really believe, and really *get* what the child is feeling. We use our affect and other SES-informed nonverbals—such as eye contact, tone of voice, and body posture—to show that we resonate with the child's feelings. In the case of the child who wants to play video games, for instance, we might lean forward, gaze intensely at them, amplify the resonance in our voice, and say, "Wow, if you think homework is boring, and your mom says you have to do it before video games, no wonder you get mad and frustrated!"

Continuing to prioritize PACE, we then communicate to the child a genuine curiosity—the kind of curiosity that transmits a message like *I really want to know what the experience is like for you*, rather than *How can I analyze this problem in order to solve it?* There is a big difference between these two approaches. Most of us can usually tell the difference between someone who centers our experience of a problem and someone who centers their desire to provide a solution. When we ask a truly curious question, we ask it without motive or judgment. We ask it in a way that allows a person to answer it however they feel, without sensing that we prefer them to go in a certain direction. In the case of the child who wants to play video games, expressing curiosity might sound like "So, hey, if you think homework is stupid and your mom keeps telling you to do it anyway, why do you think she does that?" or "What's that like for you when your mom tells you to do something you think is stupid?"

The child might respond by saying, "I hate it because then she yells at me more and I can't get away from her being mad at me" or "I don't care; I just ignore her." Regardless of the child's words, an IAFT therapist meets this response with a fresh round of acceptance, empathy, and curiosity. Offering this acceptance, empathy, and curiosity is so useful because it can disarm the child's defensiveness, helping them feel less threatened and ashamed of their inner life. It also helps uncover the child's perceptions and coping skills, potentially revealing the more vulnerable feelings underneath the problematic behavior.

Playfulness in the PACE attitude underscores the importance of inserting lighthearted, fun, warm, and silly moments into sessions wherever appropriate. Playfulness can be used to lighten a heavy moment, to create connection, to diffuse negativity, or to show a child (or a parent) that you do not take yourself too seriously. For instance, if the child says something like "I think homework is stupid, and therapy is stupid too!" you might respond with "Hey, my boss pays me a lot of money to be stupid!"

You can imagine the process of expressing the PACE attitude as a spiraled cone with the widest point at the top. At the top of the spiral sits the child's superficial behavior, the "problem" that the child is presenting. By providing acceptance, then empathy, and then a curious question (and sprinkling playfulness throughout where appropriate), you move along the spiral, generating more depth and understanding as to what lies below the presenting behavior—the underlying meaning or core issue. Each time you complete a segment of the PACE spiral, the mechanism of providing acceptance, empathy, and curiosity will generate different responses from the child. You can use this new information (whether verbal or nonverbal) to express more acceptance, empathy, and curiosity. As the cone narrows, your acceptance, empathy, and curiosity will work to uncover the deeper core issues with which the child struggles.

The Affective Reflective Dialogue and Deliberate Dialogue

IAFT makes broad use of DDP's affective reflective (AR) dialogue, which is a structured conversation that helps guide a dyad through a particular problem or situation while co-creating meaning. It is primarily used to help reestablish a connection between the child and parent that is not characterized by reactivity, or to help the child express feelings or thoughts that they are otherwise unable to articulate. In DDP, the AR dialogue relies on the therapist's intuitive sense to guide the conversation. In IAFT, the AR dialogue has been slightly modified to make it an easy-to-replicate conversation, applicable in a wide variety of contexts.

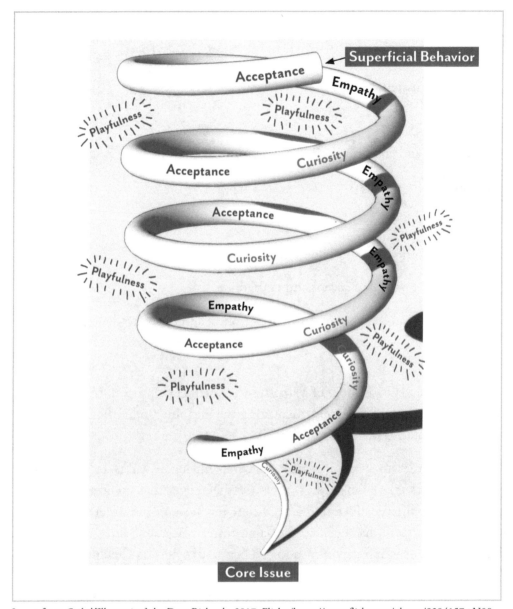

Image from *Coiled* [Illustration], by Dave Richards, 2017, Flickr (https://www.flickr.com/photos/8294157@N08 /32119735340/). Adapted with permission.

Because this conversation is used broadly in IAFT, I call it *deliberate dialogue*, and it consists of the following steps:

1. Connect and chat

2. Discuss and accept the difficulty

3. Empathize

4. Express curiosity

5. Wonder aloud

6. Get permission to guess

7. Guess

8. Validate and empathize

9. Connect to the past

10. Validate and empathize (again)

11. Facilitate the parent-child connection

12. Guide the parent to accept and empathize

13. Summarize and highlight positive attributes about the dyad

14. Problem solve

By making the dialogue more of a step-by-step, deliberate process, IAFT supports the therapist in more effectively uncovering the meaning under the behavior and in creating connection between the dyad.

It's usually easier to grasp how the deliberate dialogue works by seeing it in practice, so let's take a look at how an IAFT therapist fosters co-created meaning through a modified deliberate dialogue between Jae and his foster parents. Jae, who is 10 years old, has been in the same foster placement since the age of 4. Jae's social worker referred him and his foster parents for therapy because of Jae's episodes of inattention and anxiety. His foster parents reported that when they spoke to him, especially when they were giving directions, he tuned them out. At other times, Jae had very acute hearing and responded to conversations he overheard from the other side of the room. His foster parents felt that he sometimes acted "spacey" on purpose.

On a particularly frigid Midwestern winter day, Jae and his foster father, Mike, were out in the yard getting wood. When Mike turned around, he noticed Jae was not wearing gloves, even though it was ten degrees below zero. When Mike offered Jae his gloves, Jae would not take them. Mike expressed exasperation about this at the beginning of the session, as the therapist chatted with Jae and Mike about the cold weather.

At the emergence of this particular problem, the therapist took the opportunity to use the deliberate dialogue to explore its meaning:

1. **Connect and chat:** The first step requires connecting through conversation, showing the child that you are truly interested in them as a person. To connect with Jae about positive events in his week, the therapist said, "Hey, Jae, I know for sure the pond was frozen over this past week! Did you finally get to try on your new ice skates?"

2. **Discuss the difficulty:** The second step involves bringing up the difficult topic, using a prosodic voice to bring out the drama of the experience. This is an important opportunity to be with the child in the moment, accepting their narrative of the experience. To help Jae go back into the moment and feel those feelings and sensations, the therapist said, "Oh wow, your fingers were so cold, they were gonna fall off!"

3. **Empathize:** In the third step, empathy is used to foster and deepen connection. Empathy can be communicated through adjectives like *hard*, *uncomfortable*, *yucky*, or *not nice*, rather than categorical affect words like *sad, mad*, or *angry*. Adjectives better describe the child's state and help avoid overwhelming the child or causing them to retreat. When Jae described the incident, the therapist said, "Oh, that must have been so hard and uncomfortable!"

4. **Express curiosity:** In this step, the therapist questions aloud the reasons for the child's behavior. This allows the child to get in touch with their motives, perceptions, or beliefs about the situation. Effective expression depends on using a melodic, storytelling voice to wonder aloud about the reasons contributing to the child's choice. This voice, which we often adopt with little children, reduces defensiveness and increases engagement, even if the content is uncomfortable. At this point, the therapist said to Jae, "Hmmm, why *would* a boy be outside in the cold and have such cold hands but not be able to accept Dad's help?" It is common here for the parent to want to jump in as a problem solver. However, we want to increase the child's capacity for insight into their thoughts, beliefs, and motives. Therefore, the therapist may find it necessary to put a hand on the parent's

arm or give an understanding, acknowledging look, then say, "Oh, Dad, I know you wanted to help, but right now we're trying to figure out what it was like for Jae at that moment, so let's wait to do the problem-solving later."

5. **Wonder aloud:** At this point, the therapist uses affect to exaggerate curiosity, signaling to the child that there are valid interpretations for the child's behavior. By giving voice to the possible reasons, the therapist helps the child discover some of their motives that were previously not conscious, but in a nonthreatening way. (It is often best to avoid looking directly at the child, so as to not appear to require an answer.) Jae's therapist expressed curiosity about Jae's reasons by adopting a "thinking position," with a hand under their chin, saying, "Hmm, I wonder why? *Why* would a boy have cold hands and not take the gloves?" Usually this wondering, nondemanding tone puts a child sufficiently at ease that the therapist can then look at the child and ask, almost rhetorically, whether they have any idea as to why they reacted as they did. Jae's therapist looked at Jae and asked, "Do you know why?" The child will often respond with no, or shake their head.

6. **Get permission:** Now the therapist asks for permission to formulate a few guesses as to why the child may have responded or behaved the way that they did. Permission helps to verify that the child still wants to continue this exploration and also prepares the child for further exploration. Permission-seeking can look like the following: "Can I guess? Would that be okay?" Typically, the child will not verbally respond but will nod, shrug, or have an inquisitive look in their eye. To this, the therapist can respond, "Okay, good, I will guess."

7. **Guess:** Guesses are posed until the child signals affirmation. For example, when guessing possible interpretations for Jae's lack of gloves, the therapist said, "Could it be that the reason you couldn't use your dad's help was because you felt like you just couldn't move or say anything at all? Or could it be that you were worried that you were in trouble and taking the gloves would mean you would get in more trouble?" The therapist continued offering interpretations, posed as questions in a noncommittal, wondering tone, until Jae responded affirmatively. Such a response might look like a simple nod of the head or a moment of eye contact. Even if the therapist

does not interpret the situation exactly right, the child typically responds affirmatively if the therapist lands in the ballpark of the affective state.

8. **Validate and empathize:** In this step, it's important to validate the child for their motives and offer them empathy to reduce their shame and help them feel more accepting of their experiences. This often looks like a version of the following: "Oh, okay! Thanks for telling me that!" As in the preceding steps, the therapist's responses should be deepened and dramatized in order to let the child feel the excitement of connection. For Jae, the therapist modulated their tone of voice and its resonance, responding, "Oh my gosh! You couldn't use the help because you were afraid you were in trouble! Maybe you thought taking Dad's gloves would make you get into worse trouble! No wonder you had a hard time accepting the gloves. That makes sense!"

9. **Connect to the past:** At this point, the therapist can, if applicable, help the child make important connections that teach the child that there are reasons they behave the way they do. These reasons are based on their history and not because they are bad, stupid, or crazy. For instance, at this point in the dialogue with Jae, the therapist connected current behaviors to the past: "Maybe it's because you had to do things alone in the past, or maybe you got yelled at for making mistakes?"

10. **Empathize and validate (again):** When the child offers (often nonverbal) confirmation, the therapist expresses empathy and validation again: "Oh, that makes so much sense!"

11. **Facilitate the parent-child connection:** Once the child has been able to identify their affective response and understand it in a new context, the therapist turns to the parent. To facilitate the parent-child connection, the therapist first asks the child to communicate their feelings to their parent. If necessary, the therapist asks the child if they can speak for the child. If the child agrees, the therapist moves closer to the child's side to talk from their perspective (for more tips on speaking for the child, see appendix A). Jae's therapist completed this step by speaking for Jae: "Dad, my hands were so cold, but when you came over and saw my hands, I thought I did something wrong! I thought you would be mad at me for not taking my gloves and for not asking for help. So I couldn't take them, Dad!"

12. **Guide the parent to accept and empathize:** Crucially, the therapist then guides the parent to express empathy, actively coaching their response to elicit from them a version of the following: "Thanks for telling me, Jae. That must have been scary if your hands were so cold, and I was offering help, but you were scared you were in trouble. No wonder you couldn't answer me or do what I told you to do."

13. **Summarize and highlight positive attributes about the dyad:** As this portion of the dialogue comes to a close, the therapist can continue to talk for the child to express more themes, enabling the parent to respond with empathy and facilitating co-created meaning. But to conclude the deliberate dialogue, we zoom out, making meaning by summarizing the whole discussion in a tonal, rhythmic voice. Such a summary highlights what the child and parent may have learned about each other, as well as what the therapist has learned about them. In this case, the therapist said, "Wow, Jae, you were very courageous to tell your dad what you were feeling. And Dad, you really listened and showed Jae that you deeply understood him. You two make a good father-son team."

14. **Problem solve:** The therapist also takes the opportunity to recognize the dyad's bravery in dealing with stressful issues, to highlight the positive aspects of the parent-child relationship, and to solicit suggestions for future problem-solving. For instance, Jae's therapist said, "Because you two are a good team, I think you could brainstorm some possible solutions in case this kind of thing happens again. Jae, Dad, do you have any ideas what you might do differently now that you understand each other better?" After letting the dyad brainstorm, the therapist can also add suggestions: "Dad, when you come toward Jae and he looks worried, could you talk in a quieter voice and give him more time to respond to your offer for help?"

As the preceding example illustrates, the deliberate dialogue is a highly structured dialogue for co-creating meaning. In the case of Jae and Mike, whose attachment was relatively weak due to Jae's experience of abuse and neglect until the age of four, Jae withdrew and disconnected to avoid the fear and pain associated with his early childhood experiences. Jae's foster father, while well-meaning, believed that Jae's refusal to listen was an expression of defiance. The deliberate dialogue helped the dyad break down Jae's inchoate thoughts and associated feelings around a challenging incident, enabling him to get in touch with the feelings of panic and fear that led to his inability to respond to his dad when he sensed that he had done something wrong. The dialogue also enabled Mike to express empathy for Jae and his behavior. While one conversation cannot repair a connection, it can, when done repeatedly in IAFT sessions, pave the way for a more harmonious connection between parent and child.

The Autobiographical Narrative

In addition to fundamental tools like the PACE attitude and deliberate dialogue, IAFT therapists often use other DDP tools, such as follow-lead-follow, repair, storytelling, and guessing/wondering. IAFT adapts these tools so they can be used in sessions to maximize the sense of safety and connection between the parent and child. The specific tools and interventions used will vary depending on the needs of both the parent and the child in the dyad. These tools are synergistic and gain new or renewed value in IAFT by helping to define what safe, connected, and secure attachment relationships look and feel like.

These tools serve a number of purposes, including facilitating attunement, co-regulation, and intersubjectivity in the service of creating a sense of safety and strengthening connection. They also help the child create an autobiographical narrative. An autobiographical narrative facilitates the consolidation of the child's identity, helping the child understand who they are, why they like what they like, and why they want what they want. For this reason, the narrative is important to many attachment-based therapies. In IAFT sessions, the tools for play, parent work, and deliberate dialogue both strengthen the attachment relationship and help create the autobiographical narrative.

We all have implicit, and sometimes explicit, autobiographical narratives that help us know and understand who we are in the world. Your autobiographical narrative is the meaning you make from the events, experiences, and interactions you have had with the world. It is a story you can tell about your past in order to understand how the past affects you and shapes your experiences and identity today. Your autobiographical narrative helps you know yourself. It helps you answer the immortal question "Who am I?"

In the context of therapy, creating an autobiographical narrative requires both implicit and explicit work. A therapist does not say to a child, "Hey! Let's create an autobiographical narrative together." Rather, they use the tools described earlier to manifest for the child a coalescent autobiographical narrative that can be used to support the child's sense of self or self-concept. This is closely related to intersubjectivity. However, intersubjectivity is more like a tool—or perhaps the medium—through which the autobiographical narrative can be formed. In fact, we can think of the therapy session as an opportunity for the child to learn to experience intersubjectivity on a continuous basis, by sharing small moments and events with the therapist and parent, and co-creating meanings that can be integrated into larger narrative pieces.

To get a better sense of its foundational role, let's consider an example of a child's implicit autobiographical narrative and its contribution to development. Amir is a 2-year-old boy who is being pushed in a stroller by his mother, Dana, in the park. They see a man walking his dog. The dog is smelling the grass a safe distance away. The dog appears neither friendly nor unfriendly and is essentially ignoring the mother and child. Amir fixes his gaze on the dog and points. His mother acknowledges his efforts to communicate his perception of the dog and names it, saying, "Oh, yes, dog. Doggy."

"Woof," says Amir.

"Woof, woof," Dana responds.

Clearly, the mother and child have already had this interaction numerous times. What does this communication mean to them? What are they saying to each other? The boy is showing his interest in the dog, and he also understands that if he sits upright and fixes his gaze, his mother will join his interest and there will be further meaning-making in this game of "woof."

The mother may think this interaction represents her teaching her son things about the world, like the names of animals and the sounds they make. But for the boy, the more important experience is that he can connect to his mother fluidly as they make meaning of the world, answering all sorts of important questions, such as "Should this creature be interesting to me? Is it pleasurable, neutral, frightening, or angering?"

So far, so good.

But now the dog has taken notice of the pair as they approach, and it fixes its gaze on the moving stroller. Amir now begins to grunt and thrusts his torso forward in a clear request to approach the dog. How will his mother respond? Naturally, there is a question whether the dog is friendly to approach. It is a parent's duty to be vigilant and teach a child how to gauge whether a dog is approachable and on what terms. However, beyond that, within the parent, there is already an intersubjective experience of the general concept of "dog." Whatever Dana decides to do, a variety of attitudes and sensations will be transmitted from mother to son as Amir perceives the dog.

For instance, Dana might push the stroller past the dog, avoiding eye contact with the owner, mumbling something like "Let's not disturb the dog." Or she might turn the stroller in a different direction, saying nothing as Amir continues to crank his head over his shoulder and the dog recedes in the distance. Or she might acknowledge that the dog took notice of them and remark, "Hi, doggy, we see your tail wagging. You're a nice doggy," and continue to stroll by unpressured. Or she might say, "Oh, you want to say hi to the doggy. You love doggies! We have to ask the doggy's owner if the doggy likes to be petted."

Each of these interactions has a different consequence on the boy's psyche regarding the attitude he should take toward the concept of "dog" and toward the ongoing question of *Should I share what I notice with you, Mom?* His mom's response may give him the sense that he should be wary and not approach the dog. Or her response might suggest to him that when something ambiguous happens and his mother appears not to know how to navigate it, it is better to remove himself and not speak to her about it. If she responds differently, it may impart a friendly, relaxed manner that accepts and makes positive meaning about his interest in the dog.

The interaction matters because regardless of the particulars of the situation—such as the time of day, the amount of time spent in the encounter, or the kind of dog they've encountered—the child is receiving from his parent information about the concept of "dog." These are intersubjective experiences that the child gains, which inform his concept of what it's like to relate to a dog. Over time, the information creates meaning for the child about what a dog is. To put this in the terms of an autobiographical narrative, from this encounter and others, the child learns that *this is who I am in relation to "dog."*

We learn almost everything—and we learn almost everything about ourselves—in relationship to our caregivers. A person's autobiographical narrative is, in a way, the story of how their caregivers helped them forge a sense of self, regardless of how strong and organized, or weak and disorganized, that sense of self is. To put this another way, we each develop in a relationship, and that relationship teaches us what things in the world are, what we are in relationship to those things, and what we can and cannot share about those things. This is also how we learn which things are and are not pleasant and acceptable to share with our parents. If, for example, Amir is interested and naturally curious about the dog, but Dana discourages interaction, this may interfere with Amir's ability to form his natural opinion about dogs. He may feel that he has to hide or deny his interest in dogs when he is with his mother.

Further, if Dana chooses to pass by the dog at a distance and not fulfill Amir's wish to get up close and interact with the dog, her response to his reaction to this disappointment may impact his experience. If Amir expresses his disappointment by starting to kick, pout, cry, or whine, Dana's reaction to his response teaches him what is shareable between him and her (and subsequently between him and others). Does she ignore his complaints, giving him the silent treatment until his anger subsides? Does she admonish him with a terse statement of "Stop it" or "We can't just do everything you want"? Or does she acknowledge his displeasure in some way, either verbally ("I know, you *really* like doggy—you're mad, I know") or nonverbally (a quick sympathetic look and nod and then an attempt to distract)?

In therapy sessions, a variety of tools are used to foster the child's autobiographical narrative. In the case of Amir, we might focus on parent work. Dana, to best support her son's developing autobiographical narrative, could try to become aware of her own impact on Amir in these moments. If, for instance, she is historically frightened of dogs, thinks they are dirty, or has other negative associations, she could reflect on and become aware of this. She might then be able to choose to overcome her aversion and allow her son to interact freely to the degree possible. By the same token, if she was taught that protesting, crying, and showing disappointment is a negative trait and should be discouraged, she may also pass down this attitude toward her son, particularly if she does not become aware of this message and decide to act differently. Of course, parent awareness is a big challenge because it relies on the parent's ability to separate their own needs, wishes, feelings, and desires—including in relation to how their child should behave—from their child's needs, wishes, feelings, and desires. If the parent's stuck points are due to their own childhood wounds (as is usually the case), the therapy work proceeds in tandem with both parent-child sessions and parent-only sessions.

Ultimately, experiences of intersubjectivity contribute to a person's autobiographical narrative by establishing, or reestablishing, in relationships the meanings of objects, events, and experiences, as well as helping them define and understand what it is like to be in a relationship. IAFT is especially useful in helping develop experiences of intersubjectivity because it works at the level of nonconscious exchanges, making them conscious so as to serve a new, different narrative. IAFT is also especially useful in terms of intervention: By focusing on parent work, its tools give parents the opportunity to consciously foster functional intersubjectivity, as well as the space to revise their autobiographical narratives too.

In fact, in IAFT, our knowledge of the parent's autobiographical narrative motivates our compassion for them. This is itself therapeutic, serving as a basis for the parent to see their own childhood needs with compassion, and subsequently freeing them from the constant work of pushing away negative emotions. This often enables them to think about how they would like to respond to their child in ways that might differ from how they were raised. This ability—to separate the parent's own needs and wishes from those of their child—not only signals a stronger attunement and connection to their child but is the precondition for all future attunement and connection.

4

Preparing for the Work

While IAFT offers a powerful framework and suite of tools for providing care to children and families, implementing it can feel intimidating for parents and therapists alike. First, parents must understand and agree to the idea that they are a focus of therapy and that they will be required to engage in meaningful work on themselves. Many parents bring their child to therapy assuming that the therapist will focus on the child's behavior problems and exempt them from examination or from facing the challenges associated with change. In IAFT, this is not the case.

Second, parents also face logistic challenges, especially in terms of scheduling. The IAFT cycle typically includes four or more phases of four sessions each. Parents not only have to be available to meet for sessions with their children, but they must also arrange babysitters or childcare to accommodate the parent-only sessions. In addition, parents are asked to learn what might be a new paradigm for relating to and communicating with their child—one that relies on play, touch, and other kinds of nonverbal communication. Parents are not always accustomed to this way of communicating with their child. They may be uncomfortable with it, and sometimes they may even be opposed to it.

Luckily, with preparation and practice, most challenges can be met and overcome. In this chapter, I explain the basic elements of communicating and integrating the IAFT framework and its foundational SES-based skills. First, I explain why you should articulate a rationale—for yourself and for your clients—for integrating IAFT into your model of care. Next, I discuss the materials that you can create to introduce IAFT to parents and to help communicate various aspects of IAFT. I then provide experiential exercises that will give you an introduction to the kind of work you will engage in. Practicing these skills offers personal and professional benefits. The more comfortable you become with the experiential exercises in practice, the more you increase your resilience for the work ahead, and the more flexibly you can apply what you know in session.

Parent Agreement

Therapists, myself included, often have a strong and intuitive sense of the frameworks and tools we think will best serve our clients. However, IAFT differs in particular ways from other, more general, or more widely used frameworks and tools. Not every parent or parent-child dyad is suitable for IAFT work, and not every parent will be prepared for the commitment generally required by IAFT. This is why I recommend explaining to parents the *why*, *what*, and *how* of their participation. This includes a discussion of IAFT's focus on the use of play, parent work, and deliberate dialogue to strengthen attachment, as well as the reliance on nonverbal communication and physiologic aspects of the relationship. It also includes an explanation of your therapeutic philosophy and what makes IAFT a useful addition to your practice.

While this can and should be communicated in a conversation, it is a good idea to create an agreement for parents to read and sign. The ability to articulate professional values and beliefs in writing is useful beyond expectation-setting. It helps you anchor your therapy practice in an organized and focused way. It keeps your own *why* in sharp relief, which, in turn, helps you better see the necessary next steps in the therapeutic relationship. Putting down in writing your philosophy and correlated approach does not mean you must be rigid in your perspective or that you cannot revise your tools. In fact, IAFT prioritizes flexible implementation. Instead, a written agreement allows you to share with parents a common goal and ask them to agree on common expectations. This ultimately empowers them to join you in the work. Parents can feel reassured and a sense of respect and trust when the therapist is upfront, transparent, and explicit. While you may need or want to modify your approach later, the parent agreement offers a current expression of what you stand for and how you work.

I invite you to take some time now to pen your therapist's manifesto. "Manifesto" probably sounds unnecessarily declarative. However, this document acts as your North Star when you are trying to navigate how to work with a client or family. Consider writing by hand, rather than on the computer, to allow for a slower, more reflective approach. I recommend addressing a potential client as you write—

someone who has contacted you to learn about your therapy philosophy and the way you think therapy works best. Write down what you would like this potential client to know about you and your practice so they can decide if you are the right fit and so they can feel prepared.

The effort may feel challenging. Given the range of clients we serve, it is very easy to speak in generalities, even platitudes, about our practice and its value. But for the purposes of this exercise, challenge yourself to communicate in specific, straightforward, and concrete terms. Try not to get hung up on what you think you are or are not allowed to say. Try to clear your mind of any perceived hindrances, naysayers, fears, and self-doubt. Just for this moment, assume that you do not need to justify or defend your clinical position. You can approach this work with radical candor. Let your point of view, which you have gained through valuable experience, speak to what you have learned about therapy and about being a therapist.

To give you a sense of what this document can look like, I am sharing mine here. Feel free to use aspects of it as you see fit to do so, or not. It is my expression of what I can offer in therapy and, as both a North Star and a mission statement for IAFT, it has worked well for me.

A Letter to a Potential Client:
What You Can Expect from Family Therapy from an Attachment Perspective

Family therapy with me may be a little different from other therapy you have previously participated in. Therefore, I'd like to give you a sense of what to expect. My approach is based on attachment theory and developmental psychology. Here are some of the underlying tenets of my approach:

- **The way you were raised has an influence on your parenting style today.** I will therefore typically spend the first three sessions just with you: the parent(s). In the first session, we will talk about the attachment-focused approach and what you can expect from therapy. In the second session, we will talk more in depth about your child, their issues and problems, and your relationship with them.

In the third session, I will be asking you about your own childhood relationships with your parents and how you grew up.

- **Your child is doing the best they can and is not being mean, manipulative, depressed, or hyperactive on purpose.** It is our job to figure out what they are trying to tell us—what thoughts, feelings, experiences, and desires are underneath their behavior.

- **Your job as a parent is to first be present and understand your child.** Our goal is to first make your child feel deeply heard and understood by you, their parent. Problem-solving behavior issues will come after this first task is accomplished.

Your Role in Our Work Together

Because of your importance in your child's life, you can expect that we will meet frequently without your child. The adults will meet alone in parent-only sessions at least once after every three parent-child sessions.

Before each parent-child session, I will ask you to email me the day before with several good things and stressful things that happened in the past week or since we last met. Please keep the email short (one to two paragraphs). Please note that while I will read the email, I will not respond to its content except in the session. If you have specific questions in the email that you want help with, please schedule a separate phone session with me to go over them.

Examples of things you might write in an email include the following:

- **Good things:** Héctor played goalie in a soccer game and was super proud that he helped his team win. He also overcame a disappointment of not being able to go to the pool due to rain without a big tantrum. I gave Héctor a back rub and read him a story for several nights, and he went to sleep more cooperatively without calling me and stalling.

- **Stressful things:** Twice Héctor had a big screaming tantrum; one time he hit me because I told him he couldn't have a snack before dinner. After he calmed down, he tried to reconnect with me by asking if I would play with him, but I was really upset and I couldn't really talk to him for several hours.

What to Expect During Parent-Child Sessions

I will take the lead in guiding which topic we will be focusing on in a session. The reason for this is that when a child feels that they have to hear too many stressful themes or events at once, they shut down or get overly stressed and defensive. This is unproductive, as it replicates what is happening at home. During sessions I may have to interrupt you if you bring up too much information or too many negative themes. We will discuss how you would like me to do that when we meet in person. If you ever feel like I've slighted your authority during the session, please email me after the session and we can meet next time just the two of us. I'll adjust my way of communicating with you in session.

In our sessions, you will find that I focus on your child's inner life, not on specific behaviors. In other words, I want to discover the wishes, motives, feelings, or thoughts underlying their behavior. Rest assured that I will not take what your child says literally if they make statements like "My mom never lets me do what I want" or "My dad always punishes me and not my sister." But I will not be addressing the behavior per se. At the end of the session, if consequences, solutions, or techniques are needed, I will brainstorm with both of you about what can help.

In order to help your child express their deeper feelings, I may at times speak for your child as if I were your child. I will ask you to respond to me as if I were your child. This will allow your child to take in the feelings of empathy and acceptance that we want them to experience, without getting overwhelmed or feeling shame or defensiveness.

When I talk for your child, I will ask you to respond with acceptance, empathy, and curiosity (see the handout about PACE*). Some general examples of these kinds of responses include the following:

- I understand.

- That makes sense.

- I can see how you could feel that way.

- That must be hard.

- I'm glad to know what's on your mind.

---

* This handout, which I provide to parents along with the letter, can be found in appendix B.

- I would be sad, too, if that happened to me.

- I didn't know you felt that way before.

- I get it.

When in doubt, just say things that affirm that you are listening, such as *wow*, *uh-huh*, or *thanks for telling me*.

During these times, try to avoid giving the reasons or rationales for your side. Also try to resist the impulse to reassure your child. For example, if your child says, "I feel like you love my brother more than me," avoid saying, "That's not true—I love you just as much as your brother!" There will be time at the end for you to clarify your point of view, but we will first focus on making sure your child feels really heard and understood by you, without judgment and without your trying to change their mind.

If you don't know what to say, I'll help you. This means I'm going to coach you in session, which takes getting used to. If at any point you feel too uncomfortable, you can let me know, and we will switch to a new format. I may send your child out to sit in the waiting room and talk just with you or vice versa, or we may switch to a lighter subject or a play activity and revisit the subject at a different time.

My goal is to make the therapy as effective as possible for you and your family so you can get some relief from the suffering that is happening and begin to enjoy your child.

This agreement prepares parents for the work ahead. It also serves as a resource that parents can consult to better understand therapeutic interactions, such as when you speak for their child during session. The parent agreement is also a living document—it will change in small and even big ways as you become more experienced with implementing IAFT.

Preparatory Work for IAFT

As discussed, IAFT is a polyvagal-informed therapy where attachment is facilitated and strengthened through nonverbal, physiologic communications, as well as through attunement, co-regulation, and intersubjectivity. The therapist's most important task is to establish a sense of safety so that connection is possible. Consequently, the therapist first looks at the client's functioning, whether the child or the parent, through the question of *Does this person feel safe on a nervous system level in the presence of their caregiver (or child)*?

This means that IAFT therapists take on a somewhat different role than in other therapies less informed by polyvagal theory. In general, we assess the child's position on the autonomic ladder and use a variety of tools to co-regulate the child. For example, if a child is yelling in session or threatening to throw a toy, you would not focus on setting a limit verbally. Instead, you would think about where the child is on their autonomic ladder. How is the child's breathing, facial color, and posture? If the child is in fight-or-flight mode (in which the sympathetic branch of their vagal nerve is activated), you would focus on softening your face and using a prosodic voice. You might provide a cold drink or a cold washcloth and try to introduce rhythmic activities such as reading a book or playing soft music. If the parent tries to talk too much, either by trying to reassure or appease their child or by lecturing or reprimanding them, you would explicitly direct the parent to stop and to instead focus on accepting the child's state, offering comfort when the child is ready. You would also encourage the parent to try similar measures—a cold drink or washcloth, or taking deep belly breaths—to regulate their own nervous system during the child's stormy episode.

You can prepare for this kind of work by engaging in exercises and activities that will help you anticipate relevant in-session dynamics. For that purpose, I am going to walk you through some common exercises and activities that are designed to broaden your SES communications. While it takes time to engage in this practice, it is important to do so because these exercises are likely to provoke responses from your autonomic nervous system that can be managed for maximum connection with your client. Remember that your SES makes use of the ventral vagal nerve to strengthen connection by signaling to the other person, *I am safe, I am authentic, and you can trust me and open up to me.* Therefore, you can use these activities not only with your clients but also as an important opportunity to practice recognizing, activating, and using your own SES capacity to connect.

You laid the foundation for these exercises in chapter 2 when you mapped your nervous system. Identifying how you feel when you are moving between fight or flight (sympathetic nervous system mode) to numbness and dissociation (dorsal vagal mode) equips you to better identify where your clients are on their autonomic ladders and to guide them through understanding their own maps. Similarly, practicing the exercises and activities that follow will prepare you to use them with clients in session. Some of these, such as Peanut Butter and Jelly and The Weather Report, come from the Theraplay repertoire, and I am indebted to Phyllis Booth and Ann Jernberg for introducing them to me. Others are modified versions of the exercises included in my book with Vivien Norris, *Theraplay: A Practitioner's Guide* (2020).

These preparatory exercises and activities for SES communication offer maximum benefits when practiced with a partner with whom you are close, as well as when practiced with a variety of partners. When you do the activities with someone you care about, you gain a better sense of how the activities feel for you in a more intimate relationship. When you do the activities with five or six different people—such as a friend, colleague, child, or spouse—you experience differences depending on the partner and your dynamic with that partner. These give you an opportunity to attune and adjust to particular individuals in particular moments, just as you would in a client session. Additionally, practicing these exercises with a variety of others allows you to collect experiences for navigating and repairing things when activities go wrong. This is a frequent and unavoidable occurrence. Luckily, you can turn misattunements into opportunities for repair, which I will discuss later.

After you have tried out these activities with nonclinical partners, you can integrate them into client sessions. You might, for instance, use these exercises in an initial parent meeting to explain the concepts of polyvagal theory and acquaint them with the power of their own SES. And you will certainly use these activities within parent-child sessions to create attunement, facilitate connection, and increase cooperation.

Peanut Butter and Jelly (Voice Prosody)

As an experiential exercise, this activity helps you become more aware of the power of your voice in producing various effects on the person with whom you are in conversation. It reminds you that your pitch, tone of voice, rhythm, and melodic aspect must be woken up when you talk with people whose attention you really need to capture, whether that's because they have a hard time staying in the present or because they are fearful and need to believe that you are a trustworthy person. When used with clients, this is a fun call-and-response game that plays with voice prosody to establish an SES connection.

In this game, one partner uses their voice to say "peanut butter." Their partner then imitates their way of speaking to say "jelly." Both partners must attend to changes in volume, pitch, rhythm, and emphasis. Different variations will have different effects on both partners, partly because when the receiver attempts to produce the same voice quality back to the sender, the sender feels the effect of their communication on a physiologic level. This give and take is less about sending and receiving and more about resonance and amplification.

The game begins when you say "peanut butter" in a funny way. Your receiver responds by saying "jelly" in the same way. You go back and forth like this, emphasizing different aspects of prosody, including pitch, tone, emphasis, pauses, rhythm, or melodic aspects. There is a bit of a challenge here because *peanut butter* has four syllables and *jelly* only has two. This difference serves an important purpose: When you send a signal, you translate it through your brain, your body, and your SES. You need to make adjustments to account for differences and will not be able to mirror your partner. This is good because mirroring is not the point. A mirror is flat and provides mimicry, not responsiveness. It may sound strange, but mere mirroring or mimicry disables connection because your partner senses that you have not really heard and felt their intention.

When you first try this exercise, be mindful of resonance. Remember that resonance is the amount of vibration in your abdomen, chest, throat, and mouth. In IAFT, we use resonance to respond to somebody who feels very, very strongly about something, whether anger or sadness or excitement. We *don't* use resonance as a mirror—we don't match an angry sentiment with an angry voice. Instead, we use the vibration in our voice to indicate the sincerity of our intentions. It's this vibration-fueled sincerity that likely gave rise to expressions like "a full-throated apology."

After practicing Peanut Butter and Jelly with friends or family, try it in sessions with a child and their parent. However much you've practiced, remember that you won't always be able to anticipate the reactions of others. For instance, a child who is anxious or confused may make a mistake, like repeating "peanut butter" rather than saying "jelly," then feel embarrassed and have a dorsal vagal reaction, such as refusing to continue. Or they might have a sympathetic nervous system reaction, such as getting loud, getting up, running away, or getting silly. When this, or something similar, happens, welcome it as an opportunity for attunement and repair. Acknowledge the difficulty with a warm and empathic face and explain that the game may have been too hard and that you were not trying to trick the child. In the case of the child repeating "peanut butter" rather than saying "jelly," you can then say, "You know what? You can say 'peanut butter' back to me!"

Note that if peanut butter and jelly are not common foods in your area or in your client's culture, you can swap them out for other words. For example, in Israel it is common to say *falafel* and *pita*, while in Finland it is common to say *pannukakku* and *mansikkahillo* (pancakes and strawberry jam)!

Creating the Gaze Effect (Eye Contact)

Another important exercise to strengthen connection through the SES depends on the gaze effect. Remember that gazing at somebody is different from just looking at them. A gaze is a look that is tender, loving, and based on the felt sense that the gazer feels that the person they are looking at is special, unique, and cherished. Creating the gaze effect can be useful in a number of contexts, but it is particularly useful when working to foster connection with someone who is in distress, who is in a lot of pain, or who otherwise needs calming and presence.

When you first practice this exercise, the ideal partner will be someone you trust and who has fairly good self-regulation. This is because it is generally easier to experience the meaning and power of the gaze effect with someone with whom you already flow and with whom any necessary repair is relatively simple and straightforward.

First, together, reflect on the saying, *The eyes are the window to the soul.* Next, look into your partner's eyes, focusing on their left eye with your left eye. Left-eyeball-to-left-eyeball corresponds to right-brain-to-right-brain, so it gets you a bit closer to this emotional side of the brain. Really try to look *inside* the other person's eye, as they do the same to you. Try to imagine that as you look into their eye, you can see the flame behind their pupil that represents their soul, moving and dancing in the light. Combining these elements produces an effect in the brain, in part because when you gaze at somebody, your pupils dilate slightly. It is imperceptible to your partner's consciousness, but they can still feel it, in the sense that they feel seen, important, listened to, and valued. This is very different from being merely looked at.

It must be said that it is intense to look at another person in this way! Other than newborn babies and their parents, very fresh lovers, and psychopaths, most people do not truly gaze at one another. In fact, you may find that simply practicing this exercise causes discomfort. However, with practice it will become easier, especially if you keep the end goal in mind: to nonverbally communicate that you are an engaged listener.

Gazing is especially helpful when you feel that you are having a hard time connecting with a client. Maybe the client is defensive and caustic, or they express behaviors that trigger you and make *you* feel defensive. When you imagine that you can see this client's soul behind their eye, and focus on this flame rather than on what they're saying, you may be more capable of seeing their humanity— which can, in turn, help produce a softening in your body posture.

Practicing the gaze effect will also help you experience and understand the importance of being purposeful and present when you look at your conversational partner, regardless of the connection you may or may not have with that person. It might even remind you that being a therapist is something akin to a meditative practice, or to the practice of a dancer or an artist. With embodied practice, you can help exert an influence on another person that induces trust and cooperation.

Proprioceptive Input (Touch)

Touch is one of the elements of the SES and one of the most powerful and effective ways to transmit intention. Imagine that you and your partner are at a party, and your partner comes along next to you and puts their hand on your back. This touch can send a number of possible messages. It might indicate *I'm here to support you as you conduct this conversation with this acquaintance.* Or it might be a more aggressive signal, like *I want to control you or dominate you.* Or it could be an erotic touch, something that hearkens to an earlier romantic experience or the promise of a future caress.

Whether at a party or in session, touch can be a powerful, flexible tool for connection, for teaching about worthiness, and for producing feelings of calmness and safety. When integrated effectively, touch produces a strong bond. This is even true for adults or children who are sensitive to touch because of trauma or sensory issues. For these clients, a firm, grounding touch that facilitates proprioceptive input is incredibly useful. Proprioceptive input helps us understand where our bodies are in space. It is supplied by firm, enveloping touch—more like a deep massage or joint compression than a light or ticklish touch. Firm, enveloping touch can stimulate the nerves in the joints and tendons and under the skin to produce a calming or grounding effect in the nervous system.

Because introducing touch in therapy, even with adults, is crucial to connection, it is important that IAFT therapists become familiar with its most effective expressions. For instance, you might take someone's hand and wrap your hands around their wrist and forearm. This is a surrounding touch. It feels encompassing and grounding and can transmit signals of safety. It may be more familiar in its common form: the handshake. You offer a surrounding-touch handshake when you put your other hand over the back of the other person's hand while shaking it. This consolidating touch says, *It was really good to be with you today.*

Practice providing proprioceptive input to several people in your life. You might find opportunities to practice the surrounding-touch handshake with colleagues with whom you are not necessarily close. Take note of how you feel as you get ready to offer this kind of handshake. Consider how it is received by the other person and whether it produces any notable feelings in you or in the other person. What you notice will provide you with information about integrating this kind of handshake into sessions with the parents in your practice.

You might find that you are able to consistently transmit signals of safety with this touch. Or you might find that you prefer other kinds of touch, such as a touch on the shoulder or a fist bump. You may sometimes decide that, for reasons related to gender, age, or culture, it is not appropriate at all for you to touch a client. In this case, it is still important to support nurturing touch in other ways, as I discussed in chapter 2. You might provide a hot cup of tea, soft blankets and pillows, silky hand lotion, a cushioned footstool, or a heating pad. These all support a client's own sense of touch, enabling their connection in more indirect ways.

The Weather Report (Touch and Voice Prosody)

This important Theraplay exercise transmits a sense of calm and safety through touch and a prosodic voice that can make your partner feel almost as though they are in a trance. Practice this experiential exercise with a loved one, such as a friend, your child, your partner, or even a pet or a teddy bear.

In this exercise, your partner will turn around with their back to you. You will then describe today's weather for your location while touching their back with gestures that represent your description. Orient your play partner first by explaining that the activity will help you practice a skill that you would like to understand and learn. Let them know that it involves touch and that it will hopefully make them feel good. Also tell them that you will ask for feedback about how it felt when you are done.

Begin the exercise with a flat hand on your partner's back. Make sure all of your fingers and your thumb are firm and are providing good pressure. Then start the weather report, speaking in a soft, storytelling voice. This does not have to be the most accurate reporting, of course; it is just a story about the weather accompanied by touch that approximates the report. You might say:

So, today in Chicago, in the morning, puffy clouds filled the sky. [*Slowly moving your hands in circular motions all around their back.*] They were big, heavy clouds and they were spread out all over the sky. There was also a wind that was going back and forth, and back and forth, and back and forth. [*Sweeping your hands from side to side.*] It was moving the leaves that were on the trees and the branches that were up high in the sky, waving them back and forth. Around noon, the clouds started letting out droplets of water. [*Lightly tapping their back with your fingertips in a fluttering, downward motion.*] The gentle rain pattered down onto the roofs and windows of all the city's buildings, onto the tops of people's umbrellas, onto the windshields of their cars and buses. It sprinkled down onto the grass, the trees, and all the other plants, helping them grow. After that, the clouds began to part. [*Pressing with your palms and moving them slowly up and out, toward your partner's shoulders.*] They went up and away, and up and away, and up and away.

Duration is an important aspect of this activity: It has to last a while. It's not just that it feels good to be touched; it's also that it takes a moment for your partner to figure out—in their physiology—what the activity includes, how it is going to feel, and whether it is something they should worry about going wrong. Consider using a timer the first few times you try this exercise. Each story segment should last about 15 to 20 seconds. This is because each time you make a change, even just an auditory change, it cues a visual change for your partner's imagination, which stimulates the brain and makes them more alert.

The goal is to relax your partner, imparting a sense of calm and safety, so it is important that the activity lasts long enough to enable relaxation. In fact, as the activity goes on, and you continue using your storytelling voice and storytelling rhythm, your partner will likely become very calm and move into a trancelike state in which they are no longer worried and no longer thinking about what's going on outside of your story. You should make each segment of your report long enough for this regulating, calming effect to take place.

Throughout your weather report, you will want to be attuned to your partner and notice their body language. Do their shoulders seem relaxed? Are they wiggling, giggling, or talking? Your partner should feel that they are listening to—not participating in—a story. They do not need to chime in; if they do, it might mean that they are uncomfortable. You can check in with them by pausing and asking if they prefer different pressure or if they would like you to stop.

In session, this is an activity meant for a caregiver to do with their child. However, you may find that clients who are fearful, mistrusting, or traumatized feel uncomfortable with the idea of The Weather Report. For this reason, it is best to demonstrate the activity for all clients on a stuffed animal or pillow first. If the child is mistrusting but the parent is willing to participate in a demonstration, the child can watch as you give the parent a weather report. In this case, asking the child to follow along and practice on a stuffed animal can help make the child more comfortable and provide them a sense of mastery. After the demonstration, you can move to having the caregiver guide the activity. If it is the parent who is too anxious or dysregulated for this activity, but the child is open and willing to engage and the parent trusts you, then you can guide The Weather Report on the child.

As with all of the experiential exercises and activities, it is important to monitor nonverbal responses. If, for instance, during a weather report between parent and child, the child hunches their shoulders or starts giggling, instruct the parent to pause the activity and check in with the child. You may also suggest that the parent adjust the firmness of the touch or the speed of the movements in order to help the child relax into the activity. Once the child looks more at ease, point this out to the caregiver along with a supportive statement, such as "Okay, Dad, Tommy looks more at ease. You adjusted well to make his body calmer."

You may find that children with controlling tendencies want to ask questions or push back, such as pointing out that the description by you or their parent does not match the current weather outside. In these cases, try to continue with the story. Sometimes a child who is accustomed to talking a lot to distract themselves will settle into the experience when they notice that their questions are not necessarily going to be answered. The weather reporter should *not* pose questions to the child (e.g., "What do you think the weather is today?"). Encourage the child to simply relax and listen, allowing you to guide the activity, showing them with your confidence in the storytelling, which you communicate through voice prosody, that the experience is interesting enough for them to get absorbed.

Using the SES Activities in Session

For any of the IAFT concepts and interventions to be used effectively, they must first pass through you, the practitioner. This applies to these SES exercises too. This is why it is so important to be intimately familiar, cognitively and physiologically, with the way these activities affect you. Practicing them will help to broaden your SES, which will then prepare you to foster a deeper SES-based connection with your clients. Additionally, practicing the exercises before asking your clients to engage in them makes you more authentic and confident about applying what you have learned—which, again, enables a more meaningful connection with your clients.

I have experienced this connection myself. For example, after practicing the gaze effect, I was able to look a particular client's father in the eye. This may not sound like a victory, but I had previously felt disdain for this parent and had a difficult time meeting his eyes in session. Practicing Creating the Gaze Effect with a partner prepared me to engage in the gaze effect with this client. I was able to look at him in a way that changed my sense of him: I noticed his green eyes with brown speckles, and I focused on his left eyeball. I imagined the flame of his soul, and it softened my face visibly, from flat to warm. In the moment, I even felt like the father was becoming less loud and more tender in his voice and face.

I want to again acknowledge that some of this preparatory practice may feel strange. In fact, no matter how touchy-feely you consider yourself, I can almost guarantee that you will feel some degree of awkwardness. When those feelings arise, you do not have to push the awkwardness away. Instead, take a pause, notice how you feel in your body, and count to 10. Usually the awkwardness passes. If it does not, experiment with doing the activity on another day or with a different person. This kind of experimentation is part of the process. It will help prepare you for when you are in session and need to respond to different people and situations, so you can show each client that you really care about them.

5

Overview of the
Four Phases of IAFT

The IAFT framework is a therapeutic paradigm that balances structure with flexibility. Its course of care typically consists of three to four phases, depending on the involvement of one or two parents. Each phase includes, on average, about four sessions. Although each session follows a basic plan, the session's different components allow for a great deal of flexibility. For instance, although every session in the second phase begins with a play activity to stimulate togetherness and connection, the specific play activities are determined according to the dyad's needs or themes.

In this chapter, I discuss how IAFT's balanced approach to care supports you with a predictable structure while also empowering you with tools that can be flexibly used to build and strengthen your connection to your clients and your clients' connection to each other. This chapter provides an overview of the typical IAFT course of care. In the chapters that follow, I offer more details and illustrations about working with parents, conducting the dyad assessment, and working with the dyad. Each detail aims to foster the child's attachment security, resiliency, and sense of self through the parent and dyad.

The phases of IAFT can be—and often are—repeated, either with a second parent (as the fourth phase) or until you and your clients feel that progress toward the goals has been made. As you'll recall from chapter 1, the four phases are as follows:

- **First Phase:** Focus on the Parent

- **Second Phase:** Focus on the Parent-Child Dyad

- **Third Phase:** Specialized Focus on the Parent

- **Fourth Phase:** Focus on the Second Parent

Each phase, as I've mentioned, typically includes four sessions (sometimes five). The sessions in each phase focus on either the parent or the dyad, and each session is structured accordingly. The parent-only sessions, which I discuss further in chapter 7, often focus on attachment-based work, parent self-reflection, and guided meditation. In the dyadic sessions, which I discuss in chapter 8, the sessions include a play activity, deliberate dialogue, and another playful or nurturing activity.

Within this organizing schema, you, as the therapist, will decide which activities are most appropriate to the needs of the parent, the child, and the dyad. In general, IAFT tools are not prescriptively applied. Instead, they can and should be used in response to ongoing situations or to moments that arise in session. You are best positioned to know which tools are necessary and useful for a particular dyad, based on your knowledge of the history and challenges of that parent and child.

Despite the flexibility of their application, the IAFT exercises and activities themselves are more structured. The contrast is purposeful. Part of my motivation in developing IAFT was to avoid undue reliance on the therapist's intuition or their best sense of what a client or dyad requires. Intuition and clinical judgment are both critical to therapeutic work, but they are also honed through long and diverse session-based practice and experiences. In IAFT, the course of care and the tools are designed to support therapists as they gain the experience that will deepen their intuition and best sense. The more experience you gain, the more confident you will feel in your sense of how to modify IAFT exercises and activities to suit a particular dyad's needs.

Regardless of which IAFT tools you utilize and when, in all sessions, I encourage you to prioritize attunement, co-created meaning, and intersubjectivity.

Preparatory Work

The preceding chapters have prepared you for IAFT work by discussing the theory and therapies that inform IAFT, and by guiding you to create your own autonomic ladder and to engage in preparatory SES exercises and activities. Additionally, your experience with other attachment-based therapies will undoubtedly inform your work. This kind of specific preparatory work will better equip you to not only explain IAFT to parents, but also connect more meaningfully with parents in the initial phase and with their child in the second phase.

First Phase: *Focus on the Parent*

Session 1: Agreement and Intake

Duration: 1 to 1.5 hours

Goals:

- Review the parent agreement with the parents.
- Determine if both parents will undertake therapy or just one parent.
- Gather information about the child's developmental and trauma history.
- Ask the parents questions about what it has been like to parent their child.
- Prepare the parents for the upcoming sessions.

Before the first session with a new client, email the parents your version of the parent agreement form (which you may have written in chapter 4). This agreement acts as a social contract and guides the course of the IAFT sessions. It is therefore important to review the agreement in the initial session with the parents to ensure they understand the process and course of care. It is also important to get parental agreement to engage in the treatment as presented.

During this review, parents often request modifications. Some modifications are feasible and even necessary. For instance, it is common for parents to express frustration that the first phase is focused on them instead of the child. Sometimes a parent's sense of urgency is so intense that they feel you must see their child before the parent can even begin to engage in the IAFT course of care. As with the fight-or-flight mode of the sympathetic nervous system, the parent's urgency must subside before they can meaningfully participate in the other phases of

IAFT. In this case, it is feasible to meet the child after the first intake session with the parents so that you can assess the situation and make specific behavior recommendations or provide referrals for other evaluations. IAFT is flexible enough to accommodate this modification, and it is up to you to decide whether it is necessary.

It is also common for parents to express hesitancy about the time commitment required by IAFT, and some parents request fewer parent-only sessions. This is not typically feasible for a variety of reasons, primarily because IAFT includes a fundamental focus on parents and parent work. During the first session, as you and the parent discuss the parent agreement, you can explain which of their requested modifications can be granted and which cannot be granted and why. Mutual agreement is crucial to ensure a common understanding of expectations.

After mutually agreeing to the parent agreement, you will then gather information about the child's developmental and trauma history. Most child therapists gather this information, so you are likely already equipped with a variety of tools to this end. However, for the IAFT course of care, the details of a child's earliest developmental and trauma history are critical. These details aren't always easy to capture during intake because parents frequently gloss over pieces of information that they deem unimportant or no longer relevant (perhaps because they happened when the child was an infant). Parents might also feel that some details are too painful, so they prefer to downplay them. Because of this tendency, glossed-over details should be considered opportunities to dig deeper into the parent's memory.

For example, during one intake session, the parent described first visiting her daughter in the orphanage. She expressed a vague memory about its pristine cleanliness. When I asked her to elaborate, she initially could not remember why this stood out in her mind. However, after I asked a few prompting questions, she was able to recall that the orphanage was indeed incredibly clean, but it was because the youngest children were fed with their hands tied to their chairs, all of which had wheels. They were fed this way so they could not grab the spoon. Then, once the baby was given a spoonful, they were pushed to the back of the crowd of children to await their turn again.

For the parent, this was a small and barely recollected detail. For me, however, it indicated a traumatic and frankly cruel practice that would profoundly affect a baby's sense of agency in interacting with the feeding process. This detail was even more important for the dyad because the parent's chief concern about her daughter's behavior was her daughter's random aggression toward her siblings. Knowing that her early experiences included having her hands tied during mealtimes, which likely contributed to feelings of helplessness in getting fed enough and in an attuned way, provided a partial explanation for why this child might feel defensive when stressed by other children.

The point of this example is to illustrate the importance of intimately knowing the circumstances and stories of the child's infancy in order to better understand their current behavior. These details associated with a child's developmental and trauma history aren't always easy to elicit, but it's vital to the course of care to support the parent in their efforts to remember as much as possible.

After gathering the parent's narrative of the child's developmental and trauma history, ask the parent to describe their experience parenting their child. In IAFT, we frequently ask guiding questions that get at how effective the parent feels in guiding their child. Such questions do not typically take the form of "Why are you here?" because that encourages the parent to focus on the child's behaviors rather than the parent's experience of *being with* their child. Instead, ask directed questions such as "When your child is upset, do you feel like you understand them?" "Do you feel effective in comforting your child when they are upset?" or "Do you like spending time with your child playing games or doing activities?"

The information you gather from these questions provides you with some insight into why the parent is in session with an IAFT therapist as opposed to a behavioral therapist. It also sheds some light on the parent's own autobiographical narrative, which, in turn, will impact the autobiographical narrative that you, the parent, and the child will begin to co-create for the child to support their sense of self through the course of care. More importantly (though surprisingly little discussed), the parent's responses also open a window of compassion onto their sense of their own experiences. In fact, when you help to narrate the child's developmental and trauma history, connecting it to the parent's experience of parenting their child, the parent often begins to find space within themselves for compassion for their child. As importantly, they also begin to find space to have compassion *for themselves*. Naturally, you, as the therapist, begin to deepen the compassion you feel for the difficulties faced by the dyad. Compassion, which helps create a sense of safety and fosters a strong connection, supports all IAFT work.

In a way, this first session functions as part of the parent's early education into IAFT. During your time together, the parent passively and actively learns that IAFT is an attachment-based therapy that works to foster and strengthen safety and connection. Safety and connection begin to occur even during this session, between you and the parent, as well as between the parent and their own experience with their child. The session typically ends by preparing the parent for the next session, which will focus on parental attachment history.

While it is ideal that both parents participate in the IAFT work, this is not typical, simply because time and logistics make it challenging. Often, one parent is the primary caregiver or has more significant issues with the child that need to be addressed. If both parents do participate, determine during the first session which parent will participate in the dyadic sessions first.

Session 2: Parental Attachment History

Duration: 1 to 1.5 hours

Goals:

- Discuss the Questions for Parental Self-Reflection.
- Begin the process of making the parent aware of the connections between their attachment history and their child's attachment patterns.

Studies have demonstrated a strong relationship between an adult's attachment security and their child's attachment classification (Shah et al., 2010). But this does not mean that patterns cannot be managed and changed. To gather the baseline on which change depends, this second session proceeds from the Questions for Parental Self-Reflection developed by Siegel and Hartzell (2003) and based on the Adult Attachment Interview (George et al., 1985), a series of open-ended questions designed to collect information about the parent's childhood experiences. Many therapists are already familiar with this material, as it is critical for understanding attachment patterns. The questions include "What was it like growing up?" "Who was in your family?" "Did you feel rejected or threatened by your parents?" and "Were there experiences in your life that felt overwhelming or traumatic?" (Siegel & Hartzell, 2003, p. 133).

While the content of the parent's answers is important, so, too, is their manner of response. Are their responses coherent, detailed, and comprehensible? Or are they confusing, vague, and convoluted? Both the manner in which the parent answers the questions and the answers themselves offer deep insight into the parent's attachment capacity. You will use this information for an integrated discussion where you help make conscious the connections between the parent's responses to the Questions for Parental Self-Refection and their responses from the previous session. These connections help explain some of the dyad's current challenges with attachment. They also indicate helpful exercises for the dyad and inform the points of focus for parent-only sessions.

The insight you gain from the parent's narration of their child's developmental and trauma history, as well as their narration of their own experience raising their child and the answers they provide to the Questions for Parental Self-Reflection, should evoke your empathy, which is critical for an effective course of care. Any therapist who works with children and their parents can attest to the occasional—or perhaps even frequent—difficulty in empathizing with parents. This is especially the case when a parent appears to contribute to their child's challenges or to obstruct beneficial change. However, by asking these evocative questions, regardless of the content of the answers, we begin to see and understand the parents' experiences as children. We see that they are often products of attachment patterns that are not conscious to them. They repeat these patterns in nonconscious ways and are unable to change, even when they may want to. By offering them compassion and empathy, we model the compassion and empathy they can hold for themselves and for their children.

Session 3: Parent-Child Play Assessment with the Social Engagement Principles

Duration: 1.5 hours

Goals:

- Create a 1-hour videotaped observation of the parent-child play assessment.
- Assess the dyad's interactions and engagement.
- When appropriate, further assess the child alone.

This session offers an opportunity to assess to what extent the dyad is (and is not) in sync with each other. How does the child react to parental stimulation? How does the parent respond to their child's excitement? You will answer these and other questions using vagal match assessment (VMA) games, a foundational tool of assessment in IAFT.

VMA games include activities such as tossing a balloon or making funny faces. (I discuss the games in more detail in the next chapter.) Basically, these games are designed to allow you to observe and assess the quality of each dyad member's nervous system, as well as the quality of the dyad's nervous system interactions. By providing a context in which the variabilities of the parent's and child's differing vagal responses can manifest, the games give you insight into the quality of connection of the dyad and its general functionality. VMA games enable you to see how the dyad interacts with each other, which then informs your plan for addressing challenges and themes in future sessions.

The assessment typically consists of four to five VMA games and is videotaped. Recording the session allows you to review the dyad's interactions after your initial observation, carefully assessing parental attunement, co-regulation, and the fostering of intersubjectivity. Not only is this information crucial to developing a plan of care, but it is also useful as an educational resource, informing your efforts to foster and strengthen the dyad's connectivity and educating parents in parent-only sessions.

In dyads that include a preteen or teen, you will meet with the child alone after the VMA games. You may also meet with younger children alone, if it is merited. This determination will depend on your clinical judgment as it is informed by the material you've gathered from the VMA and the previous intake sessions. For instance, you may realize that there is an additional version of the relational story that the child would like to tell you. In this case, simply state that you would like to chat with the child alone for a bit as part of the assessment. You can ask questions such as "What would you like to tell me about yourself?" "Why do you think your parents are coming with you here?" "Do you agree with your parents about the problem or situation at home?" and "If there's one thing you would want me to know, what would that be?"

Session 4: Parent Meeting

Duration: 1 hour

Goals:

- Share with the parent your observations, connections, and assessments.

- Conceptualize with the parent the focus for the next phase of work and remind them what to expect in this phase.

- Explain the PACE attitude, model and role-play how it can be used with everyday problems, and assign the parent a trial period for using PACE.

In this parent-only session, you will continue to educate the parent on the contributions of attachment to their own and their child's autobiographical narrative. You will also provide a very general overview of vagal responses and various SES-based strategies for responding to dorsal vagal and sympathetic nervous system modes. Next, you will share the connections you see between their child's developmental and trauma history, the parent's experience raising their child, the parent's own attachment history, and your observations of the dyad during the VMA games. You may find it useful to illustrate these connections with material from the preceding sections, including excerpts from the video recording.

After making these connections conscious to the parent, you will conceptualize with the parent the next phase of work. This next phase is focused on the dyad, and each dyadic session includes opportunities for a variety of games, activities, and deliberate dialogue. The aims of the sessions in the second phase depend on your observations and assessment, as well as on parent input. For example, in the case of a parent who is angry at their child and shuts them out, the dyad may benefit from activities that give the parent supported opportunities to practice attunement and that promote the parent's ability to co-regulate. In large part, the question of focus depends on the challenges in the parent-child connection that you've observed (and shared with the parent).

Regardless of the focus, dyadic sessions will always include the use of PACE. This is a primary tool used in all parent-child relationship work in IAFT, which is why we spend at least some portion of this parent-only session explaining, modeling, and practicing PACE basics. This is typically a generative activity because responding to their child with acceptance, curiosity, empathy, and playfulness usually differs markedly from the parent's regular interactions with their child. PACE teaches the parent not to react to a superficial problem but to strive to *be with* their child. PACE also helps to activate the parent's polyvagally inflected response, enabling the parent and child to be in rhythm together.

When introducing and explaining PACE to parents, walk them through the PACE handout (in appendix B) and role-play a PACEful conversation. Here is an example role-play of a PACEful conversation with Bridget, the mother of Katie, a 12-year-old who is isolated and withdrawn at home:

THERAPIST: Okay, Mom, what would be something Katie would say that would cause an argument?

BRIDGET: When she doesn't want to leave her room and come down to join the family for dinner. I go into her room to call her for dinner, and she says, "I'm not coming. I don't want dinner anyway."

THERAPIST: Okay, Mom, would you be willing to do a practice with me? You be Katie and pretend I am you.

BRIDGET: Okay. [*Pretends to be Katie.*] I'm not coming to dinner. I don't want to eat.

THERAPIST AS BRIDGET: Oh, got it. The thought of coming to dinner isn't very appealing right now.

BRIDGET AS KATIE: Hmm. I'm staying in my room.

THERAPIST AS BRIDGET: You are cozy in here, I guess. Is there something in particular that makes it hard to come to dinner?

BRIDGET AS KATIE: Yeah, you talk too much and ask too many questions about stuff. And I hate how Alex [*Katie's brother*] always shows off and acts so stupid.

THERAPIST AS BRIDGET: Hey, I appreciate knowing what's on your mind. I hear you. I wonder if I can ask fewer questions? I'll be more mindful of that.

BRIDGET AS KATIE: I'm still not coming.

THERAPIST AS BRIDGET: I do believe you about that. If you change your mind, I would like you to join us.

THERAPIST [*signaling with their hands that the practice is over*]: What was that like for you as your daughter?

BRIDGET: I felt really closed off and like I just wanted to be left alone, but your way of being curious without arguing calmed me down somewhat. But I don't think this would work with Katie. She's not going to just cooperate and come to dinner.

THERAPIST: Would you be willing to try if I could lend you some courage? Because the aim is not necessarily for her to cooperate; it's for there to be a softening in the relationship between you two so you're not always tense and arguing.

BRIDGET: I'll try, but I'm pretty doubtful that it will help.

THERAPIST: I hear you. It's risky to even consider that this will help. But I think it's worth a shot.

As this example suggests, after you've introduced and role-played PACE, you will ask the parent to try using PACE at home. Tell them that you will check in with them in the next parent session about whether they were able to practice and how it went for them.

You will also explain that PACE supports deliberate dialogue—a step-by-step, therapist-led conversation about a difficult topic that the parent has shared with you over the course of the week. Explain that this conversation explicitly guides the parent-child connection by, in part, acting as a script for practicing PACE. It culminates in the parent's acceptance of and empathy for their child's feelings, and it closes when you help make meaning of the difficulty while problem-solving for the future.

Second Phase: *Focus on the Parent-Child Dyad*

In the second phase of IAFT, the care centers on the dyad. Most parents understand, at this point, that they must work to change their own patterns of connection if they want to benefit from IAFT. However, they also want a witness to the difficulties they have with their child. In these dyadic sessions, you are that witness. However, you are not impartial. Your therapeutic role consists of supporting the parent in taking the lead to change their own patterns—and thus the dyad's dynamic. Consequently, you play an active, responsive role, lending the dyad your whole self by, for example, energetically participating in the play portion of the session and supporting the parent in the deliberate dialogue portion. With your help, both parent and child can begin to work toward synchronization through play, while the parent learns to master the PACE attitude and deliberate dialogue. The parent also learns that their goal in IAFT is to *be with* their child, attuning to, co-regulating with, and creating moments of intersubjectivity in tandem with their child to strengthen their connection and consolidate their child's autobiographical narrative.

Sessions 1–3: Dyadic Sessions

Duration: 1 hour each

Goals:

- Facilitate structured sessions for play and reflection for the parent and child.

- Introduce and manage noncompetitive, nondidactic games to support regulated connection or relaxation.

- Provoke and support reflection focused on underlying motives rather than on superficial behaviors.

Each dyadic session follows the same basic structure: It begins with play, shifts into deliberate dialogue, and then closes with a nurturing activity. It typically looks like the following:

1. Chat

2. Play

3. Deliberate dialogue about a particular incident or challenge

4. Play

5. Wrap-up

Each session is designed to create moments of connection by fostering attunement, co-regulation, and intersubjectivity. Each session also provides opportunities for reflection in the service of co-creating meaning. This serves the creation and consolidation of the child's autobiographical narrative, which, in turn, serves the child's sense of self. Typically, moments of connection are facilitated through a combination of SES activities, such as Peanut Butter and Jelly and The Weather Report. The opportunities for reflection occur through therapist-facilitated dialogue on one or two themes using the PACE attitude. Reflection at the end of these sessions ensures that you, as the therapist, can make connections conscious for the dyad and provide useful suggestions for problem-solving. Such reflection also enables meaningful closure.

Session 4: Parent Session

Duration: 1 hour

Goals:

- Discuss the parent's feelings about and reactions to previous dyadic sessions.
- Answer questions and give recommendations about behavior problems at home.
- Practice PACE.
- Practice SES activities to improve the parent's ability to co-regulate with, attune to, and calm their child.
- Engage in a parent experiential exercise.

In the second phase, every fourth session—generally about once a month—is a parent-only session. The focus of these sessions varies, and it is often informed by the parent's strong emotions—such as frustration, anger, and hopelessness—in relationship to their child. However, the focus is also informed by your observations, as well as by insights gained from the child's developmental and trauma history, the parent's experience of raising their child, the parent's own attachment history, and the ongoing vagal interactions between the parent and child as expressed in the dyadic sessions. Additionally, it is not uncommon for the parent to simply want to talk about their own feelings about their experience in therapy.

Typically, these sessions are organized according to a discussion of the preceding issues. The session then segues into an experiential exercise, such as mapping the parent's autonomic ladder or guiding them in meditation (the latter of which I discuss in detail in chapter 7).

Depending on the parent's concerns, parent-only sessions may need to occur more frequently than once every fourth session. There is a lot of flexibility here, and some parents benefit from meeting for parent-only sessions as frequently as every other week. Ultimately, if a parent begins to express exhaustion, burnout, or frustration with the pace or progress of therapy, or a strong desire to give up, they are signaling a need for dedicated one-on-one time.

Even if one parent takes the lead in IAFT, during these parent-only meetings in the second phase, it may be helpful for the second parent to join the primary parent in order to understand what is transpiring in therapy, to provide support to the primary parent in their learning, or to work on a particular issue.

The second phase, and its attention on the dyad, does not have a conclusive end. Rather, the sequence of the second-phase sessions repeats until you and your clients feel that some or most of the goals for therapy have been met, or that an opportunity for optimal progress has been achieved. You may find that you repeat this cycle many times, or you may feel ready to advance to the next phase in just two or three cycles.

Third Phase: *Specialized Focus on the Parent*

The third phase offers an opportunity to work with the parent in four or five parent-only sessions. These sessions are helpful and necessary when a parent arrives, as almost every parent does, at a stuck point. These kinds of stuck points take many forms. For example, for a parent whose child displays rejecting behaviors, the constant rejection may bring up challenging feelings from the past associated with being out of favor with, or needing to take care of, a needy and rejecting parent. You might work closely with the parent on not getting overly upset with their child, but the parent reacts explosively over and over again. This calls for a series of parent-only sessions with a special focus on feelings associated with rejection.

To give another example, a parent who faces self-doubt because they are criticized by their spouse or extended family may need dedicated support to strengthen their inner voice about why they are choosing to parent in a different way than their spouse or the culture around them. In another instance, a parent might repeat unhelpful behaviors, such as rescuing their child from situations the parent had previously deemed necessary to help the child experience consequences and boundaries. Sometimes, these unhelpful behaviors are rooted in a parent's guilty feelings about their past parental failings, and they feel the need to compensate the child for those failures.

In all of these cases, the third phase and its focus on special issues with the parent can help the parent identify their own dynamics, acknowledge and receive empathy for them, and then separate them from the behaviors they want to show to their child going forward. Once progress toward these goals has been made, you and the parent will return to the second phase for continued dyad work. Ideally, the special focus on the parent provides the support necessary for an even stronger connection with their child.

Fourth Phase: *Focus on the Second Parent*

The fourth phase is not always a part of the course of care in IAFT. This is because the fourth phase repeats the previous three phases with the second parent. Although it is ideal to work with two parents in IAFT, this is not standard. Most of the time, given the time investment required in IAFT, only one parent is able to commit to its obligations.

Closure

Regardless of whether or not the course of care is repeated with the second parent, there a comes a time for the course to conclude. When do you know it is time to end care? One sign is that the parent and child feel closer to each other and more connected due to both the parent's and the child's deeper understanding of the child's motivations and the parent's empathy for the child's experience. This shift typically brings on improvements in the frequency, intensity, and duration of the relational problems that brought the family to therapy.

Another realistic reason for closure is when other issues emerge, such as problems in the parental marriage or relationship, or the child's need for further treatment in domains such as occupational therapy, psychiatry, or special education services, which leads to a natural end to the utility of IAFT. On other occasions, closure may be provoked by a parent's frustration with the IAFT therapist's lack of focus on behavioral fixes. This can manifest when the therapist presents the parent with a hard truth about themselves, and the parent decides to terminate therapy.

When closure occurs before it seems warranted, it's best not to see it as a therapeutic failure. As hard as it is not to take this rejection personally, your deep work and care show your investment in the family. Further, in the instance in which you communicated a hard truth that the parent found too painful to hear, that hard truth may serve as an important guidepost for the parent, and when they are ready to consider and reflect on your guidance, they may pursue your recommendations.

I have also had families whose issues seemed to subside for a time, but they later returned for a bit of a tune-up or because other issues had arisen due to a new developmental level or a change in family or life circumstances. It has been a true delight for me to continue working with families I met years—even decades—ago! For a parent, the process of attuning to and listening to their child's evolving autobiographical narrative, while striving to be in sync with them as they negotiate changing boundaries, never ends. And luckily so, because it means parents always have new opportunities to repair and connect in fresh and meaningful ways.

6

Dyad Assessment

Observation and assessment are crucial tools for IAFT therapists. They assess the parent-child dyad first, and then the parent and the child independently. They assess the energy of the interactions between the parent and child, and the attunement and co-regulation within the dyad. This information is gathered through careful observation of the parent's and the child's bodies, including the child's posture, the coloring of their skin, and their energy level in the context of their parent's same bodily communications. With these and other forms of nonverbal information, IAFT therapists consider whether the parent and child are in sync and able to communicate effectively and intuitively with one another.

Importantly, *in sync* does not always refer to an ideal relationship. A parent and child might be in sync with each other because both are shut down, or in dorsal vagal mode. In this case, the parent and child are not able to connect with the other, despite their shared nervous system experience. Accordingly, assessment serves the goal of facilitating the dyad's synchronization in a ventral vagal state, where connection can be forged because openness to others is maximized.

Because this is one of the shared goals of individual sessions and the whole course of care, assessment of the parent-child dyad is continual in IAFT and happens both informally and formally. Informal assessment is ongoing: During each session, you'll repeatedly assess whether or not—and where in the nervous system—the dyad is in or out of sync, modifying your approach and activities accordingly. A formal assessment occurs in the first phase of care. In this chapter, I will discuss the details of this assessment, as well as assessment tools, such as the Marschak interaction method (MIM)* and vagal match assessment (VMA) games. I will also discuss the particular expressions of the SES often observed in the course of assessment.

---

* MIM is part of the intellectual property of The Theraplay Institute, Chicago, IL, USA.

Marschak Interaction Method and Vagal Match Assessment

How do we assess whether a parent and child are physiologically in sync in ventral vagal mode? There are several ways. One important method, which informs the assessment tools used in IAFT, is the MIM assessment used in Theraplay. The MIM assessment is a comprehensive and rigorously structured system in which the parent and child complete nine different activities, each of which is videotaped and assessed according to preset guidelines in the dimensions of structure, engagement, nurture, and challenge.

The MIM is an accurate, useful tool in the context of assessing the parent-child relationship. It offers deep and comprehensive insight into the various ways the parent and child respond when providing and responding to structure, engaging with or avoiding one another, demonstrating or deflecting physical contact, attending to expressed and unexpressed needs, attempting mastery, handling frustrations, and more. However, its incredible utility depends on lengthy training for comprehension and implementation, and it must be applied with a disciplined and rigorous adherence to its guidelines. It is not advisable to engage with the MIM in a discretionary or modified way, as you simply will not receive its benefits.

In IAFT, we prioritize flexible assessments that offer deep insight into verbal and nonverbal relationship dynamics. During the first phase of IAFT, assessing the parent-child dyad takes place in a fluid process through the use of VMA games. VMA games are informed by the MIM, but the VMA is tightly focused on the SES and prioritizes practical implementation. It consists of four easily implementable games—Balloon Toss, Funny Faces, Lights Out, and Story Time—which makes it a very flexible option for most therapists working with parent-child dyads.

At the start of the assessment, you will prepare the parent to introduce each game and engage their child in play. However, you will not be in the room while the dyad plays the games. Rather than acting as an intermediary or witness, you instead leave the room and videotape the session. After the session is over, you will watch the videotape, observing and taking notes on the various elements of the SES expressed during the introduction to each activity, the activity itself, and the transitions from activity to activity.

Therapists who work with children do not always include an interactive play observation or corollary assessment in their overall assessment. This may be because typical methods and programs directed at caring for children focus on conceptualizing problems through a developmental lens, which frequently prioritizes the individual and verbalization. For these methods and programs, it is common for a therapist to observe and assess a child by giving them figurines in a sand tray and interpreting their constructs. Or a therapist may base assessment on interviews of the parent and the child for relevant information.

In IAFT, however, observation and assessment begin with the dyad and with the verbal and nonverbal elements that characterize the dyad's relationship dynamics. Play offers an excellent vehicle for expression of these dynamics because play often contributes to heightened and emotional circumstances that require a variety of on-the-spot responses. Interactive play is also typically characterized by periods of higher energy and engagement, followed by periods of disengagement for rest and recuperation. This rhythm offers an ideal backdrop for a wide variety of nervous system responses on the part of both parent and child.

Of course, the requirements and qualities of interactive play, and the relative rarity of it in other methods and programs, means that therapists are not always comfortable navigating this territory. If this describes you, consider referring to your autonomic ladder or spending more time practicing the SES activities described in chapter 4. These preparatory exercises offer an opportunity to practice unfamiliar elements of IAFT and will help you become more comfortable engaging with and usefully navigating SES activities, as well as your own SES responses. With practice, you will become more capable of quickly and easily navigating your own nervous system responses, which will help you be better able to guide the parent and child on a nonconscious, nervous-system-based level too.

The interactive play in IAFT assessment consists of the aforementioned VMA games, which help highlight the parent's and child's use of their SES, whether or not (and when) they are socially in sync with each other, and where they are in their autonomic ladder at various points in various interactions. The four games take about 15 minutes in total to complete, and the games should be completed in one session. Additionally, the games should be completed in the given order because the trajectory helps represent the energy shifts required in a functional parent-child relationship.

Consequently, you will have the dyad start with Balloon Toss, a high-energy and engaging game. It can work to foster connection while helping the dyad overcome some of the initial awkwardness associated with a session dedicated to observation and assessment. They will then play Lights Out, a much lower-energy game that mimics the regulation required to effectively interact with children. Story Time is next. This is less a game than an opportunity to observe attunement and intersubjectivity on the part of the parent and between the parent and child. It also provides an opportunity for the parent and child to reconnect after a perhaps too-intense experience with the previous games. The VMA games end with Funny Faces. This helps to conclude the observation and assessment component of the session with a high-energy and often highly connective activity.

You will need to provide the following supplies for the games:

- Four activity cards with instructions (see appendix C or prepare your own index cards)

- One blown-up balloon (not helium)

- Video camera (or any device with videorecording capacity) and a stand

- Written permission to videotape the session signed by your client

Before the games begin, explain to the parent and child that this assessment includes their participation in a number of games. State that you have four games you would like them to play, and give the parent the activity cards with the instructions for each game. Explain that you are videotaping the activities and reassure them that the recording is not to judge their performance or behavior, but to see how their physical movements and actions interact with each other, and that this information is important for you to be able to help them get along.

Inform the parent that the games should be played in the order indicated by the activity cards. The parent should first read the activity card's instructions, then explain the game to their child, and finally start playing the game. You can also explain to the dyad that they can take as long as they want to play the games and that playing all four games usually takes about 10 to 15 minutes. It is unnecessary to include information about finishing the games in your explanation. In fact, completion, including the parent's decisions about how to conclude each game or the child's desire to end a game, make up an important part of the assessment.

Once you've explained the process, start the video camera and leave the room. If you are unable to video record for any reason, you should still conduct the VMA. You can sit off to the side in the room to silently observe and write down notes. Tell the dyad that you will not play the activities or interact with them, and that they should act as if you were not there.

VMA Games

1. Balloon Toss

This activity will help you assess how the dyad manages excitement. You will need to provide a balloon filled with air (not helium). The activity card states: *The adult and child toss the balloon back and forth, counting how many times they can pass the balloon while keeping it from dropping on the floor.*

Tossing a balloon back and forth may initially sound prosaic. However, balloons seldom go exactly where we direct them. Consequently, this game has an element of unpredictability that can be fun and exciting. It has an element of danger because the balloon is not easily controlled and can quickly careen about in surprising directions if it is hit too hard. Additionally, a balloon makes a loud noise if popped, which some children (and some adults) find frightening. The challenge of passing it back and forth without dropping it, counting all the while, frequently increases the tension.

In this and any activity that involves movement and a goal, or any other element of very light competition, the parent and child need to work together as a team and in a sustained way. To successfully play Balloon Toss, both the parent and the child must be able to access a ventral vagal and sympathetic nervous system state. This is a blended state that allows for openness and connection while also enabling the heightened intensity and reflexive responses required when playing games with a common goal.

When a parent and child work energetically together—when they are in sync and in a blended state of ventral vagal and sympathetic nervous system activation— the parent works to support the child's regulation, and neither parent nor child quits prematurely. If, for example, the child hits the balloon too hard, the parent encourages regulation by using a prosodic, rhythmic voice to calm the child's responses. Or, if the child gets upset, perhaps because of perceived failure or stress, the parent supports regulation through nonverbal cues, such as offering a break after communicating through supportive facial expressions.

When a parent and child don't work energetically together—when they are not in sync or when they are in sync but in a dorsal vagal or sympathetic nervous system state—one or both may quit the game prematurely. Or one or both may address disappointment by adding to the dysregulation. For instance, a parent may respond to a child hitting the balloon too hard or dropping the balloon with a stern voice, an exasperated facial expression, or a contradictory message, such as complimenting them with a sarcastic tone. This can intensify dysregulation or end the game.

Unsurprisingly, parents and children can be out of sync in a variety of ways. For instance, it is common for a parent and child to interact at different energetic levels. This is the case when a child is active and running around while the parent is subdued, passive, or even frozen. Or the parent might be the active one, while the child hangs back or shuts down. A parent might also be loud and overly rambunctious, while their child looks on, stiff and nervous.

Other instances of regulation and dysregulation can occur in any of the following scenarios and combinations (and more):

Scenario	Parent	Child
Approach to the game	• Lighthearted • Competitive • Task-oriented • Supportive; helps their child succeed • Uninterested • Disengaged	• Lighthearted • Competitive • Task-oriented • Uninterested • Disengaged
Response to disappointment	• Responsive • Helps their child cope • Shows verbal or nonverbal exasperation or criticism • Bops the balloon too hard to play • Quits	• Falls on the floor • Bops the balloon too hard to play • Quits
Response to dysregulation	• Guides their child toward regulation • Admonishes their child • Teases their child • Quits	• Bops the balloon too hard to play • Quits

From our perspective as IAFT therapists, there is no "right" way to play this game. No matter how the parent and child play the game, their interactions provide the material for assessment and inform their course of care. Typically, dyads express a number of the preceding responses to the game. For the purposes of illustration, let's return to Elaine and Natasha from chapter 1. Recall that Natasha was adopted from Russia at age 9 by Elaine, an American single mother. After a very challenging few years, Elaine came to me due to her sense of their profound disconnection and disengagement.

When I first met Elaine and Natasha, I suspected, based on informal observation and my sense of their SES nonverbal communications, that they were spending some or all of their relationship in a dorsal vagal state. Both seemed shut down, although they exhibited this in different ways. I saw this more clearly during our formal assessment. In fact, the VMA helped to make clear some of the more challenging aspects of their dysregulation.

When Elaine and Natasha began to play Balloon Toss, Elaine, by way of introducing the game, picked up the balloon and handed it to Natasha. Natasha held the balloon between both hands.

"We're supposed to see how many times we can pass it," said Elaine. Natasha continued to hold it.

"You start," Elaine instructed. Natasha bopped the balloon hard toward Elaine, and it flew past Elaine's head.

"Not so hard!" Elaine said. She passed it back to Natasha, who hit the balloon past Elaine again.

"*Hey*, stop it! It says to pass it and count together!" Elaine exclaimed.

Natasha then giggled as Elaine bopped the balloon back at Natasha, hard.

"Hey! What are you doing?" Natasha cried, in mock anger.

Elaine, in a mostly joking voice, said, "See how it feels?!"

Then Elaine said, "Come on, let's just count to 10." Natasha passed the balloon gently.

Elaine started by counting "One!" and they continued to successfully pass the balloon 10 times. A few times, they had to reach together to pass the balloon. When they did this, they looked at each other and giggled with pleasure.

When they reached 10, Elaine exclaimed with satisfaction, "We did it!" But Natasha sat down, her face looking subdued again.

Elaine also sat down and asked, "That was fun, wasn't it?" Natasha shrugged. Elaine looked dejected. "Well, *I* thought it was fun."

As in many parent-child dyads, the videotape revealed that Natasha and Elaine initially experienced some dysregulation. Natasha seemed to be bopping the balloon hard on purpose, and Elaine became frustrated. However, when Elaine began to count, the rhythm of the activity helped them both become regulated. This brought them both into a ventral vagal state, which could be seen in their smiles and their reciprocal, coordinated intentions. This lasted for as long as there was physical movement and rhythm to the activity. When the game was over, Natasha went back into dorsal vagal mode as her mom asked her a question that she couldn't seem to answer.

This VMA suggested that engaging Natasha with verbal conversation over-whelmed her, which then caused Elaine to feel rejected, as indicated by her facial expressions. However, the game also indicated a way forward. As soon as there was movement and rhythm, there was reciprocity, eye contact, laughter, and smiles. This gave us a hint that initiating these types of interactions could bring both the parent and child into a more connected ventral vagal state.

2. Lights Out

Lights Out differs from Balloon Toss in that it enables the observation of a child's sense of safety and, potentially, their responses to confusion. It also offers an opportunity to observe the parent's response to the child's experience, and the parent's and child's ability to cope with stress. Lights Out is less a game than an activity, and the instructions on the activity card are simple: *The adult turns off the room's light, sits back down, and stays silent for one minute. The adult then turns the light back on.* If the room would be completely dark, turn a nightlight on beforehand so it will not be pitch black when the overhead light is off.

Because the activity card does not include any instructions to the parent about how or if to explain the activity to the child, the parent must decide for themselves what about the activity they should share. Often, the activity causes the child to feel puzzled or confused, and momentarily alert to the possibility of danger. The child's response usually stimulates the parent to provide verbal or nonverbal messages of security.

In your observation and assessment of Lights Out, consider the following:

- Does the parent say anything to prepare the child for the activity? For example, does the parent explain that they are going to turn off the light?

- Does the parent assess the room for any danger potentially associated with turning out the light? For instance, does the parent look to see how much ambient light there is from the window or underneath the door? Does the parent look around the room for obstacles in the path from the light switch to the chair?

- Does the parent initiate or help establish any physical contact with the child or increase their proximity to the child while sitting in the dark?

- How does parent establish the passing of one minute? Does the parent look at their watch, set a timer, or count aloud?

- Does the parent involve the child in measuring the passing of time?

- Does the child look worried, scared, puzzled, or angry? If so, how does the parent react?

- Does the child get up and move around, or do they freeze, become still, or hide?

- Does the child relax? For example, does the child lean back onto the couch or into the parent? Does the child close their eyes or perhaps sigh?

The answers to these questions help paint a picture of the parent and child's connectivity in times of stress. They can also indicate whether and how effectively the parent responds to their child's fear, is attuned to their child, and helps the child co-create meaning from the experience, perhaps to foster intersubjectivity. For example, let's say a parent turns off the light and notices their child's eyes darting back and forth as they start to rock back and forth. In response, the parent moves toward their child's side and holds their hand to establish comfortable closeness, and the child leans into the parent. In this scenario, the parent expresses their attunement to their child's nonverbal communication and their ability to be with their child in the child's fear. The child's body language suggests a receptivity to the proximity and a strong connection with the parent.

To illustrate a different experience of Lights Out, let's turn again to Elaine and Natasha. When Elaine read the card, she said, "Oooooh" in a worried tone.

Natasha immediately became alert. "What? What?" she asked insistently.

"It says I have to turn off the light and be quiet for one minute."

"Why?" Natasha asked, puzzled.

"I don't know," Elaine responded with embarrassment. As she got up to turn off the light, Elaine tripped a bit on the table leg. She laughed embarrassedly, but Natasha didn't react. Natasha was perfectly still. Elaine turned the light off and returned to her seat. Natasha looked bored. She looked down at her nails and picked at them. After a few seconds, she looked up at Elaine and asked, "Why are we doing this?"

Elaine put her finger to her lips in a *shhh* motion. Natasha looked down again and then put her head on the table. The minute passed as Elaine smiled awkwardly, looked at Natasha (who did not look at her), and then got up to turn the light back on. Natasha raised her head from her arms and had a totally flat look on her face.

Elaine said, "That was weird, wasn't it?"

Natasha shrugged but didn't say anything.

Their VMA showed that Natasha was hypervigilant to her mom's assessment of distress. She went from a dorsal vagal to a sympathetic nervous system state, asking her mom questions to get context and reassurance. However, Elaine seemed preoccupied with the task at hand. Natasha signaled again that she wanted reassurance when she asked why they were doing this, but Elaine seemed unable to connect with Natasha without using words and simply signaled for her to be quiet. Natasha immediately shut down, and there was a sense of sadness as Elaine tried to connect with Natasha during the minute of silence. There was no physical contact between them or other nonverbal connection. When the task was over, Natasha seemed more remote than before the task began.

3. Story Time

Story Time, similar to Lights Out, is less a game than an activity. It allows for an observation of the parent's representation of the child's autobiographical narrative. This helps provide a picture of the dyad's story—in particular, the parent's sense of it. The activity card reads, *The adult tells the child about a memory from the child's past.*

Questions to consider when observing this activity include the following:

- Does the parent easily recall a story?

- What story does the parent choose in terms of theme? Happy, exciting, frightening, dramatic?

- Does the story capture the situation from the child's point of view? Does the parent work to embody the child's perspective, or is the story mostly a narrative of the parent's perspective?

- Are there any themes of teasing, sarcasm, or derogation in the story?

- Does the child seem interested in the story?

- Is the child embarrassed by the story? If so, how does the parent adjust or respond to the display of that embarrassment?

- How many questions does the parent ask the child in relation to the story? For instance, is it more of a back-and-forth dialogue or a mutually constructed story? Does the parent seem to quiz the child on how much or what they remember about the story?

- Is there any touch or physical proximity during the story?

Story Time offers broad insight into the dyad and into the parent's sense of the child's autobiographical narrative, as well as the child's own experience of their autobiographical narrative. To get a better sense of this, consider Elaine and Natasha's experience.

Story Time began for Elaine and Natasha when Elaine appeared to read the activity card. Elaine glanced up, looking blank and a little scared. She glanced around the room and then sideways at Natasha. "What favorite story do we have?" she posed to Natasha.

"Huh?" Natasha responded with a blank look as she played with the tassels on her boots.

"We don't have a lot to choose from," Elaine said nervously. "Do you remember when you had just arrived in America and we went to the zoo?"

Natasha stared forward and didn't respond.

Elaine continued, "You went up to the window and the huge momma ape ran right up to you and you got scared?"

"I don't remember," Natasha mumbled.

"Yes, you do! You fell backward and laughed! We just talked about that the other day."

Natasha continued to stare blankly. Elaine sighed in an exasperated way and rolled her eyes.

"Well, I remember," she said dejectedly.

As with Balloon Toss, when Elaine asked a question of Natasha, it provoked a denial and a refusal of verbal participation, which suggested Natasha was shut down and in a dorsal vagal state. She offered no eye contact and expressed flat affect. Elaine, meanwhile, expressed nervousness and also spoke with flat affect. She asked questions in an interrogatory rather than prosodic tone, and this seemed to shut down Natasha further.

4. Funny Faces

Funny Faces is the last in the sequence of VMA games. It is a high-energy game that provides an opportunity to observe the level and tone of cooperation between the parent and child. It also helps give expression to the parent's and child's willingness to participate in what can be considered a challenging game, at least in terms of regulation. The activity card reads: *First, the adult makes a funny or silly face at their child and asks their child to copy it. Next, the adult and child switch roles: The child makes a face and the adult copies it.*

As with Balloon Toss, Funny Faces features elements that may feel uncomfortable or even threatening to some children and some parents. Specifically, the game requires direct eye contact and the unguarded expression of silliness. Again, there is no "right" way to play this game, but for its successful completion, the dyad must usually already share a sense of safety, which typically comes from a cooperative, connected place. For instance, a father and his child may start tentatively, with the dad sticking out his tongue and crossing his eyes, while the child giggles nervously and looks around the room, seemingly unsure what to do. It takes a few minutes of exchanging faces for this dyad to begin to comfortably express silliness together. By the end of the game, the child not only makes funny faces, but lends their whole body to the effort, and both parent and child dissolve in laughter as the dad attempts to follow his child's lead.

Question to consider when observing and assessing this activity include the following:

- Is the parent able to make silly or funny faces?

- Is the parent too uncomfortable to begin playing the game?

- Is the child reluctant or unwilling to follow the parent's lead? If so, how does the parent react to the child's reluctance or unwillingness?

- If the child is initially embarrassed, is the parent able to lighten the mood or coax the child into play or make the child feel more relaxed?

- Are the parent and child able to engage in enough eye contact to make the game possible?

- Does the game involve facial expressions, or are body movements and posture included?

- Does the activity produce laughter?

- Is the dyad able to sustain the activity for more than one round, or do they finish it very quickly?

Returning to Elaine and Natasha, when Elaine read the card, she immediately said, "Oh, I've got it—my Tiger impression" (referring to the family cat). She pressed her face back with her hands, stretching her eyes sideways and making a snorting sound. Natasha laughed spontaneously. Her eyes remained animated, and she appeared eager to see Elaine do the impression again. Elaine repeated the funny face and sound, and Natasha laughed again.

Then Elaine said, "Now you copy." Natasha giggled nervously and put her hand to her face, but she stopped short of making the Tiger face. She remained quiet.

"Come on, you do it at home!" said Elaine.

"Nooo, I can't!" Natasha whined.

"Yes, you can. You just don't want to."

Natasha giggled and said "nooo" again.

Elaine rolled her eyes and said, "Now I'm supposed to copy you."

Natasha looked at Elaine, then put her face in her arm on the table and giggled.

"Now you try!" Elaine urged.

Natasha raised her head momentarily and stuck out her tongue, then put her head in her arm on the table again.

Elaine stuck her tongue out, then said, "See? You have to look at me!"

Natasha peeked out for a second from under her sleeve but then hid her face again.

"Let's do the next one," Elaine said in a resigned voice.

This game revealed that Elaine had a spontaneous, confident, joyful side that Natasha couldn't help but respond to. However, Natasha shut down when she was put on the spot; this caused Elaine to become agitated, and she seemed to feel rejected. She prodded and cajoled Natasha, rather than respecting her embarrassment and noticing that Natasha was trying to participate on her own terms. This shut Natasha down further. The recording raised the possibility that Elaine could not register her daughter's enjoyment and her desire to join in with Elaine. It indicated the importance of pointing out to Elaine that Natasha wanted to enjoy her, as well as the importance of helping Elaine to not feel so rejected. The dyad's future focus would be on helping Elaine initiate more playful interactions without expecting full reciprocity from Natasha.

Assessing and Observing Patterns of Autonomic Engagement

The VMA activities are simple but effective tools that illuminate verbal and nonverbal responses within the parent-child dyad. This is because the activities encourage both the parent and child to move up and down the autonomic ladder. In doing so, the games also help motivate the individuals' SES, thereby underscoring the strengths and weaknesses of the dyad's ventral vagal connections. In fact, as suggested in the previous descriptions of each activity, a major part of the VMA assessment includes observing and assessing the dyad's SES expressions.

Recall that the SES is demonstrated through the following:

- Voice prosody and resonance

- Gestures and postures

- Eye contact and touch or proximity

When observing voice prosody for assessment purposes, listen for the rhythm of the parent's voice and consider whether it matches their child's states at various points during the VMA games. You will begin your observation and assessment of prosody as soon as the parent begins to introduce the game to their child. When giving instructions, does the parent use clear, brief sentences so the child knows what to do next and what is expected? Alternatively, does the parent use rambling, run-on sentences that leave the child confused about what to do? Or does the parent, like Elaine, assume the child knows what to do and more or less dispense with any real instructions at all?

Later, if the child becomes upset during the game, how does the parent react? When, for instance, their child is visibly angry or frustrated, flailing their arms, yelling, or gasping in big heaving breaths, how does the parent use their voice to respond? Does the parent's response convey sympathy in some way? Or does the parent use a meek or flat voice, or speak weakly or without conviction? Does the parent, like Elaine, try to nervously persuade their child of some element of the game, perhaps in order to stop an expression of frustration, or does the parent respond to their child with a strong and confident but open tone, allowing their child to feel frustrated?

When observing gestures and postures, look for the coordination of the movements between parent and child. If the child is energetic and bouncy, does the parent also have energy in their body—perhaps bouncing their knee, swaying their arms, or using gestures that match the child's rhythm? Alternatively, does the parent seem stiff and rigid? Does the parent sit down and abstain from moving with or toward their child, or does the parent only engage with halfhearted movements while their child bounces off the walls?

When it comes to eye contact, observe whether and when the parent and child look at each other. Do they reference each other when talking, looking at each other when they are trying to make meaning during play or when they have to decide who goes first in a game or activity? During Lights Out, in particular, do the parent and child look at each other to make meaning nonverbally and share connection?

Eye contact varies by culture and context, and this must be taken into consideration. It's also important to consider how variations in neurodiversity will impact the frequency and length of eye contact. For instance, a person with autism may prefer not to look at their intersubjective partner for long moments, especially when they are trying to articulate a thought or tell a story. Despite these variations, most children will still reference their parent for safety, connection, and joy.

In terms of touch and proximity, how close are the parent and child sitting to each other? Are they at arm's reach or closer? Do they need to lean and strain a great deal in order to touch? Is there any touch, even if incidental (like reaching over the other person to get something on the other side of them and touching their arm, leg, or shoulder)? Does the parent touch the child to signify or amplify something humorous? As a way of connecting? To make their point or to calm their child during a moment of stress? Does the touch only seem instrumental, or does it also appear to be intended for connection or pleasure?

By attending to their SES expressions as the parent and child engage in interactive play, you will begin to see patterns of engagement. To ensure you capture these patterns, it is incredibly useful to plot them on an autonomic ladder for each game, creating a timeline that lends itself to visual analysis. Here is the template I use (which is also included in appendix D):

	Balloon Toss	Lights Out	Story Time	Funny Faces
Ventral Sympathetic (V-S)				
Ventral Dorsal (V-D)				
Sympathetic				
Dorsal				

The graph is labeled with the names of the VMA games along the X axis and the polyvagal states along the Y axis. Notice how the ventral portion is divided into subparts: ventral-sympathetic (V-S) and ventral-dorsal (V-D). The line separating V-S and V-D represents a client who is in a neutral but ventral vagal state. A client in this state is connected, open, and engaged, but also calm and composed.

The vertical lines represent the passing of time of the activities, typically in approximately 30-second or 1-minute increments. When you are ready to plot a dyad's VMA, begin playing back the video and start a timer when the dyad starts their VMA games. On the graph, mark where on the autonomic ladder the parent and child begin, writing a P to indicate the parent's vagal position and a C to indicate the child's vagal position. As you watch the rest of the video, continue to record the dyad's positions at each time interval.

Once the VMA video is complete, connect the Ps together to form one line and the Cs another. Then consider the following questions:

- Is there a lot of up and down in the parent line over time?

- Is there a lot of up and down in the child line over time?

- Do the parent line and child line go up and down together?

- Do the parent line and child line diverge? When?

Let's take a look at the VMA autonomic timeline for Elaine and Natasha as an example:

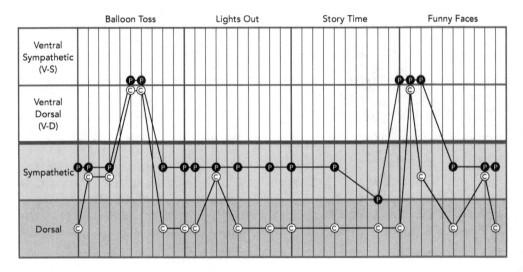

Their graph reveals some patterns. Elaine spent a lot of time in a sympathetic nervous system state—she seemed to be anxious and often prodded her daughter. Natasha could quickly match Elaine's sympathetic nervous system activation but spent more time in the dorsal vagal range. The two were at times quite similar in where they were in the VMA, but not in a functional sense. They are able to be in a ventral vagal state together when Elaine initiated lively, playful, and rhythmic activities. This suggests that with the right interventions, the dyad can have a more connected, comfortable experience.

Plotting the relational dynamics between Elaine and Natasha makes it clear that they will benefit from activities and exercises that foster Elaine's attunement to and co-regulation with Natasha, as well as Elaine's ability to support Natasha's intersubjectivity. However, both Elaine and Natasha need support and guidance to enter and maintain ventral vagal functioning, where attunement, co-regulation, and intersubjectivity can be fostered.

Once you have conducted your clients' VMA, considered the various aspects of their SES, and plotted their autonomic ladders across the activities, it is time to consider what of this information you will share with the parent in the last session of the first phase. As I previously emphasized, it can be extremely useful to show the parent a clip and ask them what they see, how they felt during the interaction, and how they think their child was feeling. By soliciting this information and sharing your specific impressions and recommendations, you bolster the sense of a team approach toward a common goal.

For example, in Elaine and Natasha's case, before I shared my impressions and recommendations with Elaine, I cued up the video to the moment when Natasha hit the balloon hard and it flew past Elaine's face. I asked Elaine what she saw and felt at that moment. Elaine said that Natasha often thwarts Elaine's attempts to be playful by ruining or shutting down the game. I empathized with Elaine and then suggested an additional reason that may be motivating Natasha's response: She was anxious and excited, and was therefore dysregulated in her movements. I pointed out that when Elaine started simply passing the balloon, adding rhythm to her passes by counting them aloud, Natasha cooperated. I told Elaine that working on adding rhythm to their interactions to increase regulation was one goal of our work together. Although Elaine considered my alternate explanation and goal, I could see hesitation on her face. She was not convinced. I asked her what her reaction was to my conceptualization, and she expressed her skepticism. I thanked Elaine for her openness with me and reassured her that it was okay if she did not agree with all of my suggestions. I also let her know that we would be revisiting all of these themes as the course of care unfolded.

Ultimately, the VMA games are an efficient mechanism for stimulating the verbal and nonverbal expressions characterizing the parent-child dyad. By using the games to assess the dyad's interactions, we learn where a dyad is out of sync and what kind of therapeutic support can help bring about more functional communication. As illustrated by the interactions between Elaine and Natasha, the games can help facilitate synchronization in a ventral vagal state, offering a means of assessment through which connection can be strengthened.

7

Working with Parents in Parent-Only Sessions

One of the most important decisions a therapist makes is how broadly to define the problem that the client brings into treatment. Our individualistic culture seems to encourage therapists to narrowly focus on whomever is exhibiting the problem behavior, without understanding the wider family context that may be shaping other issues. But often the key to working effectively with a family is expanding the therapeutic perspective to include the history of intergenerational trauma that underlies the present-day issues, even though that's not the family's view of the origins of the presenting problem. This is the course we take in IAFT, and it is not always easy to introduce to our clients.

When parents bring their child for therapy, they don't expect or want to be as much the focus of work as their child. Parents often feel that they have already expended their energy and effort in working to parent their child. They may feel ready to hand off that work to a professional. Yet, as discussed in previous chapters, one of the first things I explain to parents when introducing my method of therapy is that because I work from an attachment perspective, I will be working as much—and sometimes more—with them.

As an IAFT therapist, you will spend a substantial amount of time with the parent, getting to know their attachment history and helping them feel, as their child should, your presence as a secure base and source for comfort and hope in the therapy process. This is because IAFT, as a relational therapy, positions the parent-child dyad as the most important relationship in a child's life and considers the attachment that connects parent and child as the key to healthy development. Through understanding a parent's attachment classification, you enable a deeper, more compassionate perspective on why the parent may behave in a certain way. You will share this information with the parent, providing empathy and psychoeducation, as well as opportunities to practice attunement, co-regulation, and intersubjectivity, to support their efforts to connect with their child.

In parent-only sessions, you will remind the parent that you will be asking them to look into their own childhood history and how it may be contributing to the situation with their child. You will also remind them that the role of the parent in IAFT sessions is both critical and challenging. For all of us, our own lifetime of intersubjective experience results in a nonconscious understanding of ourselves and others, as well as a nonconscious understanding of ourselves *in relationship to* others, including our own children. This understanding manifests in ideas and expectations that we may have, even though we are not aware why we have them. For instance, a parent may want their child to be cooperative because their own parents discouraged them from speaking their needs. Or a parent may want their child to advance in school because they felt academically inferior, and they want their child to redeem their own self-worth.

While some parents are put off by this information, it is important to express confidence in the approach so parents feel motivated to give attachment-centered family therapy, with its focus on parent-only sessions, a try. When parents really and truly understand their role in IAFT, the real work of strengthening connection begins.

Questions for Parental Self-Reflection and Attachment Patterns

As introduced in the overview of IAFT, the parent-only sessions are structured by the Questions for Parental Self-Reflection (Siegel & Hartzell, 2003, pp. 133–134):

1. What was it like growing up? Who was in your family?

2. How did you get along with your parents early in your childhood? How did the relationship evolve throughout your youth and up until the present time?

3. How did your relationship with your mother and father differ and how were they similar? Are there ways in which you try to be like, or try not to be like, each of your parents?

4. Did you ever feel rejected or threatened by your parents? Were there other experiences you had that felt overwhelming or traumatizing in your life, during childhood or beyond? Do any of these experiences still feel very much alive? Do they continue to influence your life?

5. How did your parents discipline you as a child? What impact did that have on your childhood, and how do you feel it affects your role as a parent now?

6. Do you recall your earliest separations from your parents? What was it like? Did you ever have prolonged separations from your parents?

7. Did anyone significant in your life die during your childhood, or later in your life? What was that like for you at the time, and how does that loss affect you now?

8. How did your parents communicate with you when you were happy and excited? Did they join with you in your enthusiasm? When you were distressed or unhappy as a child, what would happen? Did your father and mother respond differently to you during these emotional times? How?

9. Was there anyone else besides your parents in your childhood who took care of you? What was that relationship like for you? What happened to those individuals? What is it like for you when you let others take care of your child now?

10. If you had difficult times during your childhood, were there positive relationships in or outside of your home that you could depend on during those times? How do you feel those connections benefited you then, and how might they help you now?

11. How have your childhood experiences influenced your relationships with others as an adult? Do you find yourself trying *not* to behave in certain ways because of what happened to you as a child? Do you have patterns of behavior that you'd like to alter but have difficulty changing?

12. What impact do you think your childhood has had on your adult life in general, including the ways in which you think of yourself and the ways you relate to your children? What would you like to change about the way you understand yourself and relate to others?

A parent's responses to the preceding questions convey explicit and implicit information about their attachment patterns. Explicit information includes the specific content of the responses, which generally provides enough information to understand the gist of the parent's early relationships and their attachment pattern. These patterns typically take the form of secure, dismissive, or preoccupied.

Secure or Autonomous Adults

Secure or autonomous adults tend to offer answers that explain the various ways they value attachment relationships. These parents are generally able to coherently describe attachment-related experiences, including difficult experiences such as being sick and needing comfort, or losing an important relationship because of death, moving away, family rifts, or a divorce. For example, here is how Marta, a parent with secure attachment, described a loss she experienced in childhood:

> I was very close to my grandparents. I stayed at their house so often before I was 7 that most of my memories from that time are from their house. I remember my grandpa liked to garden so much, and I loved helping him plant seeds and watching the plants grow. We did a lot together. Then my mom got a job in a different state and we had to move. My mom didn't really help me adjust to my new neighborhood and school. She was wrapped up in her work. I was pretty lost and felt lonely for what seemed like forever after we moved away from my grandparents. Yes, we saw them on holidays, but it wasn't the same. I remember when my mom and I were pulling out of their driveway the day after Christmas—I felt like a knife went through my heart, I was so sad. I wanted to jump out of the moving car and run back to them. They were just so important to me, and I wanted to see them every day.

We can easily see how much Marta valued the relationship with her grandparents. She does not idealize her grandparents or her mother. She also does not deny the negative impact she experienced as a consequence of the move. On the contrary, she speaks about how much she missed her prior relationship to her grandparents when that relationship changed.

Dismissive Adults

Dismissive adults tend to devalue the importance of attachment relationships. Or they may idealize their parents, but they are unable to give any examples of their parents' goodness. For example, here is another parent's response regarding a loss during childhood, this time from Denzel, who is classified as dismissive:

> I wouldn't call it a loss, really, because my dad left before I was 2, and we hardly saw him, so I didn't really know him. I didn't have a relationship with him, and neither did anyone else in my family, really. Then, when I was 7, we moved away from the town where the rest of our family was, so my dad's absence just didn't affect me that much. My family's hometown was so poor and run-down, there wasn't much to miss.

Denzel describes what might otherwise be considered significant losses—of both a parent and a family network—as, essentially, no big deal. The relationship between Denzel and his dad is narrated as unimportant and unimpactful. He seems to imply that the freedom involved in moving from his hometown and his father was more important than the relationships he may have had in and to his town, as well as to his father.

Preoccupied Adults

Preoccupied adults are usually still very much involved with their past attachment experiences and are not able to explore them productively. They often express anger when discussing their current relationships with their parents. Jules, a parent who could be classified as preoccupied, offered the following response when asked about their childhood experiences of loss:

> My aunt was so important to me; she practically raised me. My dad wasn't in the picture, and my mom was too busy with her boyfriend to even be around. Then he moved halfway across the country, and my mom took me away from the only home I knew so she could be with him. She's still exactly like that—she doesn't think of me or my circumstances. She'll call me, supposedly to ask how I am, but then she ends up telling me a long list of what is wrong with her life. I get so fed up! It's like she can never look at things from someone else's point of view.

Preoccupied adults, like dismissing adults, are considered to have insecure attachment patterns. These patterns are often characterized by a lack of trust, which can be attributed to a fear of abandonment. Parents with preoccupied attachment patterns might seem to be overly sensitive to those with whom they are in relationships and may therefore jump to conclusions about the reasons for the other person's behaviors or actions.

Eliciting Implicit and Explicit Themes

Determining a parent's attachment style is useful for a variety of reasons. Parents frequently repeat the behaviors that characterize (and reinforce) their attachment style. Partly as a consequence, their children can inherit or develop these same patterns. In this way, a parent with an insecure, dismissive attachment style may repeat the associated behaviors, encouraging a dismissive attachment relationship with their child. This dyad might be unwilling and unable to prioritize their relationship with one another in conscious or nonconscious ways.

In parent-only sessions, we use the explicit themes that emerge from the parent's responses to the Questions for Parental Self-Reflection to help the parent draw connections between their experiences as a child and their experiences with their child. For instance, I might say to the parent, "You were taught to be really quiet and stay in the background because there was already so much trouble in your family. Now, you have a child who is really loud, so it makes sense that you would be having a hard time engaging with a child who is so overt and attention-seeking." These connections often enable the parent to externalize their internal experiences, making them more capable of reflecting on these experiences and learning from them.

In addition to the explicit information provided by parents in response to the self-reflection, parents also convey a lot of implicit information. This is nonverbal, nonconscious information, often communicated by the SES, and includes voice, gestures, and speaking style. Through implicit information, we gain insight about the parent's experiences, their comfort level in discussing and reflecting on their experiences, their sense of their relationship with their child, and their sense of how their relationship with their child has been impacted by their past experiences and relationships. The knowledge and skill necessary for understanding the implicit meaning in the Adult Attachment Interview is an important area of study but outside the scope of this book. I urge you to read more on the subject (see, for example, Steele & Steele, 2008).

The most important consequence of the implicit information we gain from parent answers is the empathy for the parent it engenders. I have already mentioned how important empathy is to effective work in IAFT: Therapeutic compassion is a crucial component of IAFT because it enables the parent to view themselves with a similar compassion. In fact, empathy and compassion allow us to reach the parent as, in some ways, a vulnerable child too.

Regardless of whether the parent responds to the questions by rambling, speaking incoherently, avoiding the questions, refusing to reflect, using euphemisms, or even staying awkwardly silent, we see the parent as a human being with their own experiences, their own relationships, and their own associated challenges. It is not the case that the parent is at fault for "messing up" their child, though parents sometimes enter the session feeling this way. It is instead the case that the parent has faced challenges that have made safely and securely connecting with their child particularly difficult.

Because attachment is such an important part of working with parents, let's revisit Amir and his mother from chapter 3 for further illustration. In fact, Amir arrived in session as an 11-year-old with "anger issues." His anger, which was often directed toward his mother, appeared to be circumstantial and related to disappointments about video games or school. As attachment therapists, IAFT therapists see value in investigating what Amir's anger toward his mother means from a relational perspective. Consequently, after the assessment, I worked with Amir's mother, Dana, to understand the nonconscious elements of her attachment history, which she may have been inadvertently passing to Amir.

As I guided Dana through Siegel's questions, it became clear that, growing up, she was taught that the world was dangerous and that she should hold in her fear or other strong negative emotions. She talked about her parents instilling in her a suspicion of dogs and other animals, of talking to strangers, of calling attention to herself, and of generally "getting into trouble." Her parents would not voice their displeasure out loud but would feel it and express it in other ways. Dana agreed that these attitudes caused her some degree of loneliness and disconnection, as well as causing her to feel that she should not express herself or strive to get her needs met.

Now, as an adult, Dana showed indications of a dismissive or avoidant attachment pattern. She adhered to a number of different rules, and she expected Amir to adhere to these rules too. For example, when Amir was a toddler, he was not allowed to interact with dogs or strangers. Now, as an 11-year-old, he was not allowed to go over to a friend's house when he wanted to because it might be an imposition on the family, and he could not play video games with friends before completing his homework, even on weekends. When Amir responded to these rules with anger, Dana would react to his protests by ignoring him and disallowing any associated negative emotions. She also refused to allow any pushback on the unspoken rules—there was no negotiation or discussion, and there never had been. When Amir was younger, Dana denied the anger and sadness he tried to express when he wasn't allowed to interact with others in ways he wanted to. Now that Amir was older, Dana demanded that he not be angry that he couldn't play video games before doing his homework.

When Amir did get loud and protest, Dana resorted to yelling and ultimately storming away from him in disgust. When talking about this in a parent-only session, Dana expressed surprise that she so often yelled at Amir, because she said her parents didn't yell at her at all. I suggested to her that it may be because she grew up with parents who instilled in her a fear of expressing her negative emotions, and if that were the case, it was not surprising that she would react to Amir's loud emotions by attempting to tamp them down, by discouraging him from talking about them, and by ultimately ignoring him. Because Amir often yelled and protested anyway, Dana felt pushed beyond her limits. She reported feeling trapped and out of control, which is why she believed she turned to yelling and threats.

Proceeding from an attachment perspective, I explained that Dana's reactions to Amir were part of a pattern. When negative emotions are present in childhood, as they naturally are, and the child is given the message that those emotions are not okay to show, the child (and in this case, the child could be Dana *or* Amir) will try to suppress or ignore them. For Dana, suppressing her emotions worked. However, she also grew up feeling lonely and disconnected. For Amir, suppressing his emotions did not work, perhaps because he was naturally more expressive. With her more expressive son, Dana's old coping skills no longer worked—she could not continue to successfully suppress her feelings. She instead expressed explosive anger and yelled. Ignoring bad feelings and exploding or yelling are two sides of the same coin of an avoidant attachment pattern that is passed down if it remains nonconscious.

It was useful for Dana to understand the *why* behind her attachment patterns. When her patterns and their underlying origins became conscious to her, it also helped motivate my compassion. This compassion, as suggested earlier, was therapeutic because it served as a basis for Dana's ability to see herself, and her own childhood needs, with compassion. Such compassion can subsequently free a parent like Dana from the constant work of pushing away negative emotions, giving her newfound freedom to think about how she would like to respond to her child in ways that might differ from how she was raised. This ability—to separate her own needs and wishes from those of her child—not only signals a stronger attunement and connection to her child but provides the foundation for her ability to be even more attuned and connected to Amir in the future.

Once this foundational attachment work has been completed with the parent in parent-only sessions, it offers a stable launching point for you to illustrate how the tools of IAFT, such as the PACE attitude and deliberate dialogue, can help the parent consider more carefully some of their own perspectives so they can be more open to hearing things from their child's point of view.

However, and inevitably, a parent's own wishes, needs, and motives will be expressed during sessions. These might be expressed verbally, as when parents try to defend themselves. Dana, for instance, often expressed exasperation with what she considered to be Amir's laziness and wished he were a different, more motivated child. Or it might be expressed when a parent provides logical reasons for their rules. Dana often explained that Amir was not allowed to play video games before completing his homework because video games were too stimulating and caused him to lose focus. A parent's wishes, needs, and motives might also be expressed nonverbally, as when parents become stiff and distant, sigh, roll their eyes, or cross their arms across their chests. Dana frequently communicated with all of these nonverbal expressions.

As IAFT therapists, we work to prioritize the parent's experience by helping externalize it, by stopping and pointing out that the parent seems stressed, and by asking if they would like to take a break or have a drink of water. When a parent grows agitated, or responds to suggestions by rolling their eyes and looking away, you might check in by asking if they feel sufficiently comfortable proceeding with the dialogue, or if they would they like to change the format of the session and speak with you alone while their child plays in the waiting room.

Despite your efforts, there will typically come a time within the therapy process when you and the parent feel as though you've hit a stuck point. Maybe the parent feels increasingly dissatisfied with the therapy, perhaps because of the pace or because the interventions do not feel sufficient. Maybe the parent seems to no longer be listening to suggestions, or repeatedly reports, "I tried it, and it didn't work," or seems to be unwilling to identify their own behaviors or patterns as a contributor to the dyad's problems.

In the case of Dana, she reached a stuck point when she was able to provide acceptance of and empathy for Amir's disregard for school and homework during dyadic sessions, but revealed during parent-only sessions that, at home, she repeated the negative pattern of admonishing, yelling, and finally storming away from Amir in disgust. During these parent-only sessions, she also expressed growing frustration that the dyadic sessions were not helping Amir be more cooperative. She identified this as the reason she could not approach Amir in a more PACEful way at home.

The following section explores a key tool that you can use to help parents who have reached this type of impasse: guided meditation.

Guided Meditation

When it becomes clear that a parent feels stuck, guided meditation is a useful and necessary tool. Guided meditation is used by therapists in a number of ways, but in IAFT, we use it when a parent has become increasingly activated in a discussion about their child's behavior. This technique can help the parent become less reactive to the challenges posed by their child. This lower reactivity, in turn, typically allows the parent to be more present with their child. Accordingly, when parent-only sessions begin to feel stressful—for you or for the parent—or when a parent shows signs of feeling dysregulated, you can use guided meditation to help restore regulation and a sense of calm.

Guided meditation typically follows a 10-step process:

1. The parent creates a list of their child's problem behaviors.

2. The parent clusters behaviors according to their similarity.

3. The parent visualizes the behavior to identify what aggravates them the most, noting their physical sensations.

4. The parent explains what they say *about themselves* when the behavior occurs.

5. The parent identifies the core belief underlying their self-talk.

6. The parent identifies a formative past experience in which they experienced this belief.

7. The parent visualizes the experience, noting their physical sensations.

8. The therapist connects the parent's past experience and their present experience, pointing out the automatic nature of our nervous system responses.

9. The therapist guides the parent through a three-step meditation for observing feelings without judgment.

10. The therapist guides the parent through a self-compassion visualization.

Typically, you introduce the parent to the guided meditation by explaining that you'd like to help the parent see and reflect on the connections between their child's experiences, their experiences of their child, and their own experiences as a child. You might use the following script, modifying it as necessary for your own and your client's needs:

> We have talked about a number of behaviors or problems your child has that you want help with. I'd like you to take a piece of paper and write down four or five behaviors that bother you, frustrate you, or make you the angriest. These are the things that may make you feel exhausted and like you want to give up. Take your time thinking about these.

Give the parent as much time as they need to create the list. If they can't come up with five behaviors, that's okay. If they have more than five, that's okay too. Continue when the parent indicates they are finished.

> Look at the items you listed. Are any of them similar or connected? Draw the same shape next to behaviors that seem connected. Is there a common denominator? Maybe it's about disrespecting you or not seeing you as a person—anything that makes these issues seem like they have the same root cause.

If the parent can't find any similarities, take two or three minutes to look at the items the parent wrote and help the parent explore whether some of the behaviors are related. Related behaviors make up a cluster. Once the clusters have been identified, proceed with the next portion of the work.

> Which of these clusters bothers you the most? Let's focus on that. Think of a specific incident of this behavior. Now, I want you to think very specifically about that incident. Bring it back in your mind, and hold it in your mind. I'm going to ask you a few things about the experience as if you were in that moment. Close your eyes if you need to, and draw the image up in your head. Take some time to recall how you were feeling.

When the parent indicates that they are visualizing the incident, ask the following questions.

> What do you say to yourself in the moments that the behavior is happening? What does your inner voice say to yourself at that moment?

Parents will often start by saying what they think about the child: "He's never going to stop." "He's doing this on purpose." Ask the question again, emphasizing that you are specifically asking what the parent thinks *about themselves*. If they need help, clarify:

> What do you tell yourself about yourself as a parent? What does this mean about you as a parent?

After working through this question, have them write down the troubling questions that arise. Typically, these are variations of "Why don't I have what it takes to make this better?" Once they have written down a few questions, proceed.

> Put yourself back in that moment. What feeling do you have in your body when you are in that situation? Where does the stress, tension, tingling, or heat reside in your body?

If they struggle to identify their feelings, walk them through a body scan to support their awareness. Ultimately, you are working toward seeing and understanding the negative core beliefs with which the parent struggles. Core beliefs are our central ideas about ourselves, and they can be accurate and positive, or inaccurate and negative. In IAFT, by becoming aware of the feelings that arise in their body, and connecting those feelings to the intensity of their experience in that moment, the parent is often able to identify the negative core beliefs provoked by interacting with their child when their child displays certain behaviors. Common examples of negative core beliefs include:

- I'm going to die.
- I want to hurt my child.
- I feel out of control.
- I hate my child.
- I'm a bad person.
- I'm a failure.
- I'm a bad parent.
- I can't protect my child.
- I'm trapped.

- It will be this way forever.
- I will lose everything I love.
- I'm alone.
- No one will ever help me.
- No one cares about me.
- My needs aren't important.
- I don't care.
- I can't feel anything.

Once the parent has identified their negative core belief, proceed with the next question.

> Have you been through a similar experience before? When is the first time you can remember a similar feeling or thought?

If they can remember a similar situation from their childhood, let them know that there is likely a connection between that situation and the specific behavior in their child that causes them such distress, hampering their ability to stay regulated. If they can't remember or are unable to make a connection, let them know that your guess is that they may have been in a similar situation in their childhood. But don't push it. It is important to simply let them know that there is a reason why they may lose control or become dissociated or ineffectual around certain behaviors. Then, guide them to more substantive connection.

Think of another time now: the first you can remember when you had a feeling similar to this feeling with your child. A lot of times, the things that stress us the most are things we experienced in our earlier lives that have a similar flavor. We may get the same feeling of overwhelm, like we can't cope, or it takes us into strong feelings of anger or withdrawal. If you have that earlier incident in your mind, the first thing I want you to note is that the physical symptoms you are experiencing reflect an automatic nervous system response, and it's not your fault.

When you feel overtaken by powerful negative feelings, overwhelmed, or disconnected, or when you feel rage or shame, those are automatic responses in your nervous system. They are not in your control and can feel frightening, so you may respond by checking out or getting angry. But these responses can and will pass. This is not a failure on your part—it is a survival mechanism that served a function at another time in your life. There is nothing wrong with you. You can get back to a better, more present state of mind if you gently ride out the pain. You can do that in three steps:

1. Pay attention to the feeling you have in your body and focus on it without judgment.

2. Identify the negative thought that comes into your head and acknowledge it without becoming attached to believing it.

3. Take four belly breaths—inhaling for a count of 7 and exhaling for a count of 8.

Are you willing to practice this with me?

If they are willing, walk them through each step.

Now I will be asking you to think about that past experience and to try extending yourself self-compassion through a visualization exercise.

1. Close your eyes, if you feel comfortable with that, or choose a focal point in the room to look at.

2. Conjure up the incident in your head and give me a thumbs up when you are picturing the incident.

3. Tune into your body and focus on the feeling in your body.

4. Now picture some type of traveling vessel or container, like a floating bubble, a boat, a rocket ship, or any other item that moves. I like to use the image of a bubble because it is light and floats easily. Find an image that works for you.

5. Imagine sending this vessel to the area in your body where you feel the uncomfortable sensation (such as tightness or tingling). When the vessel arrives at that location, imagine it opening and letting out a message of self-compassion. The message of self-compassion that this vessel carries could be "This is not your fault," "You didn't do this on purpose," or "You are not a bad person—it is your nervous system's way of trying to protect you, trying to keep you safe."

6. Now, I will guide us both in taking three deep breaths on a 7-8 count—a 7-count inhale and an 8-count exhale.

7. When you are ready, open your eyes.

Process this experience with the parent, and if appropriate, offer some context.

We just practiced bringing together the experience of feeling stress, strain, and tension; an awareness of your body and how you feel; and loving messages of self-compassion. Combining these things with this breathing technique teaches your autonomic nervous system that it can move through strong feelings by using breath as a tool. You can exercise your mind this way to help you pass through stressful times at home, teaching your body to calm down so you can be available to your child.

In practice, this may look a little different. For example, when I conducted this meditation with Dana, she said she became angry, critical, and frustrated with Amir's negativity about school and homework. When visualizing an incident of this behavior, she realized she felt frightened of Amir's strong emotions and desires. These feelings suggested that she was in danger and was scared that something catastrophic was going to happen.

Dana expressed that these types of feelings made her feel just as she did when she was a small child. Back then, her parents often seemed to warn her, both verbally and nonverbally, that bad and dangerous things can happen if people get angry. She felt that she was always somehow in danger—or about to be in danger—and that she must be careful to not anger others in case something terrible happened.

When she imagined the incident of Amir refusing to do his homework, she realized that it provoked a bodily panic, a danger, and a sense that the world was going to end. She felt paralyzed and unable to move, a feeling that was especially noticeable in what she described as her frozen shoulders. She also reported experiencing a kind of tingling, along with shallow breathing and surges of energy, that made her feel that she needed to act.

I pointed out that her current feelings about Amir's behaviors were likely related to patterns she had learned from past experiences. Her own conduct—admonishing, ignoring, yelling, and finally storming away in disgust—was associated with coping mechanisms that she learned a long time ago in order to survive in her family. Her conduct today suggested how important it had once been to suppress negativity because she had learned that negativity could be dangerous and even life-threatening.

At this point in the guided meditation process, Dana and I breathed deeply together, and I let 15 to 30 seconds pass to encourage regulation. I encouraged her to feel and accept her feelings, to allow all of her feelings, even the uncomfortable ones, to be okay. This was challenging, but it was important. Her ability to tolerate her feelings of doom, even for a few seconds, enabled her to also tolerate feelings of self-compassion.

Next, we brainstormed a message of self-compassion that she could use to counter the message that she was in danger. I typically use the following list of negative and positive cognitions (PESI, 2022) to guide my suggestions.

Negative and Corresponding Positive Cognitions	
Control/Choice	
I do not have control of my life.	I am in control of my life.
I am weak.	I am strong.
I am powerless.	I am capable.
I cannot succeed.	I can succeed.
I will fail.	I can handle it.
Safety/Vulnerability	
I am in danger.	I am safe now.
I cannot stick up for myself.	I can trust my judgment.
I can't trust anybody.	I can choose whom to trust.
I can't trust myself.	I can trust myself.
I cannot protect myself.	I can take care of myself.
Perfectionism/Self-defectiveness	
I should be better.	I did everything that I could.
I did something wrong.	I learned from the situation.
I should have done more.	I did my best.
I should have known better.	I can't blame myself for what happened.
I should be more like X.	I don't need to compare myself to anyone else.
Responsibility	
I am not worthy.	I am worthy.
I am stupid.	I am intelligent.
I deserve to die.	I deserve to live.
I am insignificant.	I am significant.
I am a bad person.	I deserve to be loved.

Although Dana identified "I can take care of myself" as an appropriate message of self-compassion, she clearly struggled to believe this, or even to accept it as a message of self-compassion that could apply to her. However, as with building her tolerance for feeling painful feelings, it was necessary to continue to work in parent-only sessions to build her tolerance for feeling positive feelings. Though she was clearly uncomfortable, wincing and shifting at several different points, I pointed out that simply trying to deliver messages of self-compassion was enough.

It is important to point out here that parents will not always voice their discomfort. Just as we attune to our child clients, we must also attune to our parent clients. With parents, however, we can point out that we notice their discomfort, and we can emphasize that trying to offer self-compassion is sufficient. It is not necessary that they believe their message of self-compassion to build their capacity to feel it.

My guided meditation with Dana concluded with some nice, easy breaths together. When she opened her eyes, I asked her how she felt. She reported feeling a little confused, a little unsure if she was doing things the right way, and a little skeptical. But she also said that she felt her body, especially her shoulders and back, were more relaxed. She reported that she had not previously seen herself and her relationship to her parents as so closely connected to her relationship with Amir. She hadn't considered when or why she had felt the same feelings that she felt in response to Amir's behaviors. She hadn't thought about how her own feelings of fear and panic contributed to Amir's responses. She also hadn't realized how hard it was to feel painful feelings, or positive ones.

Guided meditation is an important piece of IAFT parent-only sessions. It should be integrated as a regular part of these sessions, in part because, by practicing self-compassion, parents become capable of connecting with themselves and self-regulating their various responses to uncomfortable emotions. By learning to better regulate themselves, parents learn how to better navigate their relationships with others, and this includes their children.

Parents usually have an inherent sense of what their child needs, if that sense is not blocked by their own dysregulation. Working with parents in this iterative way typically stimulates a gradual shift in the parent's mind that can support greater regulation. However, guided meditation is critical for another reason too. Although it does not necessarily contribute to the child's autobiographical narrative, it can in some ways stand as a short and simple autobiographical narrative and meaning-making tool for the parent. The repeated process teaches the parent how to make peace with their own difficult experiences so as to foster peace with their child.

8

Working with Children in Dyadic Sessions

While the parent-only sessions are critical to the success of IAFT, the dyadic sessions are the heart of our work. During these sessions, we focus on fostering and strengthening dyadic connection through attunement, co-regulation, and intersubjectivity. This requires forging links at different levels—between therapist and child, between therapist and parent, and within the child through their understanding of their autobiographical narrative. To facilitate the connection required for the child's attachment security, resiliency, and sense of self, we also prioritize safety. Ultimately, we establish a sense of safety so we can better connect with the child and the parent, teaching the parent to connect with the child and supporting the parent-child connection.

During the dyadic sessions, we forge these connections by giving our whole self to the child, modeling for both child and parent the connective power of attunement, co-regulation, and intersubjectivity. Although each dyadic session will unspool a bit differently, depending on the client, the context, the themes, and the shifting in-session dynamics, you will usually organize dyadic sessions according to a common structure: beginning with play, shifting into deliberate dialogue, and then closing with a nurturing activity.

In this chapter, I explain how a typical dyadic session works through the example of a session between Whitney and her daughter, Maya. I provide information from the intake and parent-only sessions to show how these closely inform the dyadic sessions. Although Whitney and Maya face their own unique challenges, their relationship was strengthened over the IAFT course of care in important and characteristic ways.

Whitney and Maya: Intake and Parental Attachment History

Maya, who was 13 years old, was having trouble getting up to go to school and often missed the bus. During the intake process, Maya's mom, Whitney, revealed that she and Maya's dad had recently divorced after several failed attempts at reconciling their marital problems. Twice in the last year, Maya's dad had moved out for a period of several months and stayed with friends. Later, Whitney and the children moved in with Whitney's mother, where they were currently living. Whitney revealed that the marital problems included emotional abuse, wherein Ethan called Whitney names and threatened her with violence. During parent-only sessions, when Whitney spoke about her own childhood history, she described a similar pattern between her parents, where her dad would bully her mom and intermittently rage at her and her sisters. Whitney said she developed an eating disorder when she was 12 and had to be hospitalized twice for being dangerously underweight. Her anorexia was successfully treated through therapy that was provided to her through school.

During the first phase of IAFT, as part of the agreement and intake, Whitney also reported that she was diagnosed with depression and was on antidepressants until age 22, when she met and married Ethan. She got off the antidepressants because she felt happy and because she wanted to get pregnant and was afraid the medication would interfere with the baby's development. Whitney felt that in the first few years after Maya and her younger sister, Tamar, were born, they were happy as a family. After that point, Whitney began suspecting that Ethan was having extramarital affairs. He vehemently denied this, and they fought over Ethan staying out late into the night. Whitney realized she would have to become more independent of Ethan, so she pursued night school to become an accounting assistant.

Whitney said she had always been excellent at math and gotten almost perfect scores in high school despite her depression and eating disorder. She successfully graduated from the accounting program and got a high-paying job in a private firm. However, with all the stress of her failing marriage and subsequently dealing with Maya's school refusal, Whitney missed too many workdays and was ultimately fired from her position.

This caused Whitney to fall into a serious bout of depression—she cried a lot, was despondent, and didn't get out of bed for several weeks. This affected Maya, who showed symptoms of anxiety (chewing her hair and nails, and having fears about going to school) and depression (not wanting to get out of bed or go to gymnastics). During this time, Maya called her maternal grandmother, who came to help take care of Maya and Tamar. Whitney went back on antidepressants, which helped her to keep up with her daily routine more effectively. Although Whitney felt better and wanted to start looking for work again, Maya's refusal to go to school kept her too occupied. Whitney had a meeting with the school counselor and the social worker; Maya was supposed to attend as well, but she refused to go. During the meeting, the counselor and the social worker told Whitney that they believed Maya's school refusal was a "family system issue" and recommended they go to a family therapist together.

During the intake, the IAFT therapist asked Whitney what she thought the counselor and the social worker meant about it being a family systems issue. According to Whitney, she was told that she gave Maya mixed messages about going to school. Whitney expressed anger because she felt the counselor was unnecessarily blaming her for Maya's behavior. Maya, during the intake, said she didn't want to go to school because she found school boring, stupid, and useless. Maya also said that her mom wanted her to get good grades and go to university for engineering, accounting, or another field where she could earn good money, but that she was not interested in university. Further, Maya stated, "My mom goes back to bed after I leave for school, so she can't tell me what to do anyway."

When therapy began, Maya had missed over 50 percent of the school year. Whitney tried threatening, cajoling, bribing, and physical force to get Maya to go to school. They often got into loud, painful arguments where Maya would say hurtful things and Whitney would also say things she later regretted. For instance, Whitney once told Maya that it was Maya's fault that Whitney lost her high-paying job because she'd had to attend to Maya's school problems.

During the parent-only sessions, Whitney grappled with feeling a tremendous amount of confusion about her relationship with Maya. She felt that she didn't understand and could not help or control her daughter. Her sole goal as a parent was to give her daughter a better life than she had, and she was worried she had made a terrible mistake—both by leaving her marriage and by not leaving soon enough. At other times, she commented on how much better Maya had it than she ever did and how Maya needed to toughen up. Indeed, Whitney generally reported that she believed that people should not complain and that talking about their negative feelings kept them focused on the past. She saw this as a weakness. She also felt that other people (the school staff and Maya in particular) were blaming her for Maya's school refusal.

Once these parent-only sessions were complete, the focus shifted to the dyadic relationship, where the goal was to facilitate joy and connection between Whitney and Maya. Here I discuss the structure of dyadic sessions more generally and then explore specific interventions used when working with Whitney and Maya.

Dyadic Sessions

Dyadic sessions are designed to create connection by fostering attunement, co-regulation, and intersubjectivity, and by providing opportunities for reflection in the service of co-creating meaning. This serves the creation of the child's autobiographical narrative. The trajectory is actualized through the session's structure:

1. Chat

2. Play

3. Deliberate dialogue about a particular incident or challenge

4. Play

5. Wrap-up

During the session, the IAFT therapist works to attune to the child and mediate between parent and child. In this case, mediation does not mean brokering agreement or finding compromise. Instead, mediation serves as a tool that lets you model for the parent what healthy in-sync connection looks like. For this reason, you will take a strong lead throughout the dyadic sessions, offering your whole body—in your state of ventral vagal social engagement—to connect with both parent and child and to facilitate the parent-child connection.

At the beginning of each session, engage your clients in a few minutes of initial chatting to establish a connection and to communicate that you care about their lives beyond the clinic's walls. Then segue into the session's play portion.

Each dyad will play different games, depending on their need. It is up to you to determine—based on information from the intake and the parental attachment history, as well as the parent-only sessions—which games will best foster and support dyadic connection for that particular parent and child.

I've discussed games in previous chapters, and more are described in the upcoming paragraphs. There is a wide variety of games; however, all of the activities in the IAFT spirit have the following attributes in common:

1. The activities are not intellectual, academic, or focused on strategy. Instead, they are focused on fun, joy, laughter, and silliness.

2. The activities are not competitive but cooperative (such as a relay race or passing a ball), with the adult helping the child.

3. The activities are tailored to the child's developmental level so that they can, with just a little bit of effort, succeed and feel proud.

4. The activities involve some type of movement or rhythm (such as singing, clapping, stomping, snapping, swaying, rocking, or marching) to engage more aspects of the SES.

5. The activities help the dyad connect and encourage working together and making eye contact to achieve a goal.

6. The activities involve touch, even if the touch is indirect (for example, a game in which pillows are stacked on the child's back while they're lying down, providing light pressure).

While these guidelines are important, what is even more important is how you—as the IAFT therapist—initiate, model, and lead these activities. Your role in leading games and activities includes the following:

1. Take responsibility for clearly and simply explaining the rules of the activity.

2. Make sure that no one gets hurt. This includes clearing obstacles that could cause injury. If someone does get hurt, stop, check in with that person, offer them comfort (such as a bandage, a drink, or a gentle pat of reassurance), and then adjust the activity or the space to prevent the injury from happening again.

3. Keep the activity regulated and in a comfortable zone. It's okay for a child or parent to get excited, but if their enthusiasm becomes over-the-top (for example, jumping off the couch) someone could get hurt. If this happens, address it, and modify the activity to make it more comfortable.

4. Join in the activity as both a guide and a participant, demonstrating with your SES that it is pleasurable and safe to have fun, be joyful, and act silly with another person.

5. Be prepared to nurture a child (or parent) who has an attachment need. This means having supplies ready to offer, such as blankets if someone is cold, a fan or ice water if someone is hot, lotion if their hands are dry, bandages if they are injured, snacks and water if they are hungry or thirsty, or any other element of comfort that a client might have that can be reasonably facilitated.

As in the other elements of the session, you will actively and energetically participate in the play portion of the dyadic session. Typically, this ensures the games are fun, stay noncompetitive, and provide a way for the parent and child to connect.

For Whitney and Maya, the choice of activities used to begin the dyadic sessions was influenced by Whitney's anxious, driven, and focused demeanor. Whitney was very logical and serious, and her tone was pressured when speaking, as if she were demanding an answer. In the dyadic sessions, one of the big goals was to loosen Whitney up, help her be spontaneous, encourage her to move fluidly, and enable her to share her smiles and laughter with Maya. Additionally, the mother and daughter did not usually share touch or connect through affection, so another goal was to support this capacity. Activities were therefore chosen to allow for caretaking opportunities and to create natural opportunities for touch, while not requiring any overt intimacy.

Maya's general lack of energy also informed the choice of activities and games. Maya was not a particularly lively child. She often showed up to appointments looking lethargic and she usually remained slumped on the couch throughout. To establish the safety and comfort on which successful play depends, it was important to not physically tax Maya or require or expect too much enthusiasm. At the same time, Maya had a funny, sarcastic, and playful sense of humor, which was a different kind of energy, and it often came out in spurts, surprising both her therapist and her mom.

With these considerations in mind, Whitney and Maya typically played one of the following games during the play portion of the dyadic sessions (for more games and activities, see Norris & Lender, 2020).

Candy Guess

During this game, Maya closed her eyes, then Whitney gave Maya a small piece of chewy candy and asked Maya to guess the flavor. Next, they switched roles: Maya gave Whitney a small piece of chewy candy to guess the flavor of. Then Maya did the same thing with the therapist.

Feather Dartboard

In this game, Whitney held a feather while Maya acted as the dartboard. Whitney announced where on Maya she would blow the feather, such as her knee, hand, head, or shoulder. Then Whitney tried to blow the feather so that it landed there. The inevitable failure to aim the feather is usually a part of the game's hilarity. Once Whitney finished her attempt, they switched places: Maya directed the feather while Whitney acted as the dartboard. Once Whitney and Maya had both had a turn, the therapist took a turn too.

Song Lyric Game

This game particularly interested Maya and Whitney because they both liked music and had very diverse and eclectic musical tastes. In this game, Maya said a word from a lyric of a song—such as *sunshine*, *love*, or *rain*—and Whitney had to think of songs with that word in it and then sing the song phrase. If Maya had a song in mind that Whitney did not mention, then Maya would get a point. As with the other games, everyone took a turn.

Play-Doh Guess

In this game, Whitney, Maya, and the therapist each took a piece of modeling clay and sculpted it into a figure or shape. Then they guessed the others' figures.

When Maya was feeling more energetic and was willing to stand up, the group played more active games, such as the following.

Add to It

Whitney, Maya, and the therapist took turns making a movement while the others copied it. In the next round, a second movement was added to the first, and the sequence was then copied. In the third round, a third movement was added to the sequence and the whole sequence was then copied, and so on.

Meowish

Maya had a childish side that was younger than her chronologic age of 13. She had her own cat language and knew how to speak cat. She would make various cat sounds and meows, and Whitney and the therapist had to take their best guesses at interpreting the meaning.

During some dyadic sessions, Maya (or Whitney) would be too upset or dejected to play and interact with the other. In these cases, Maya used a notebook that was kept in the office for her for just this purpose to write down what she was feeling. When Maya refused to participate in this way, she could usually be persuaded to draw hieroglyphics that represented her feelings. This ended up becoming a ritual—each week, Maya would show the hieroglyphics she had written the previous week to see if her mom and therapist could figure out what she had been feeling.

After approximately 20 minutes of playing a few of these types of games, the next portion of the dyadic session begins. This is often the most challenging portion because during this time, you will guide the parent in a deliberate dialogue with the child about an issue or problem. Typically, this gives the parent a chance to receive supported practice using a consciously PACEful attitude.

In preparation for talking, set up the room for maximum comfort. This might mean adjusting the lights and offering heavy blankets and big pillows or something smaller, like a fidget item. If you've followed the IAFT phases, then by this point the parent has already been introduced to and has had a chance to use the PACE attitude and practice engaging in deliberate dialogue. However, this prior preparation does not mean that the parent does not need support. These conversations are often difficult for both parent and child. You should step in as much as necessary to slow down the conversation, foster regulation for both parent and child, and model PACE. You may also need to speak for the child, with the child's permission.

Handling a Child Who Refuses to Talk

Because it happens so frequently, it is important to prepare for dyadic sessions in which the child will not talk. This is especially common in initial efforts to foster open and in-sync deliberate dialogue between the parent and child about challenging topics. These kinds of conversations are often unfamiliar to the parent and child, and both are usually stuck in prior patterns that may be marked by dysregulation and disconnection. When a child refuses to talk, their parent frequently tries to intervene, admonishing their child or trying to answer for them. During the session, it is important to point out to the parent that this is not helpful and to then model a different response.

There are a number of ways to respond to a child who refuses to talk, including:

- Letting them hide under a blanket or pillow

- Giving them something to clutch, like a big teddy bear or pillow

- Not asking for verbal confirmation

- Asking if you can guess their response, and for them to give you a thumbs up or down, or a toe up or down, to indicate whether you're right or wrong

- If they don't answer you, wondering out loud to yourself or to a stuffed animal in the room

- Supporting the child in "not knowing"

It is also important to recognize that nonverbal responses—such as shoulder shrugs, an intense gaze, a shift of the head, or looking down—are responses. When their child is an infant, an attentive parent notices not only their baby's screaming or squealing, but also any wiggling or squirming, the color and temperature of their baby's skin, the fluidity of their baby's movements, the dilation or constriction of their baby's pupils, and the rhythm of their baby's breathing. In the same way, you should look at the child (and the parent) for nonverbal signs of communication.

You can and should also support the child in not knowing. This means responding to their "I don't know" with enthusiasm: "Thank you so much for telling me you don't know. It's okay not to know. It makes total sense. There are so many times when I don't know why I am feeling a certain way or why I did something!" Because the goal is establishing a sense of safety so as to foster and strengthen connection, your support allows the child to feel safe in not knowing.

Sometimes a child will push back, saying (or shouting), "I don't want to talk about it!" At times like these, you have to decide what's at issue: Is it that the child doesn't *want* to talk but can still tolerate talking if you strongly support regulation and communicate a true sense of safety? Or is the child really and truly becoming overwhelmed and dysregulated? For example, a child who doesn't want to talk but can tolerate talking might cover their ears and sing to themselves, "Hmm, hmm, hmm, I'm not listening," while a child who is becoming overwhelmed and dysregulated might clutch their ears forcefully, groaning and yelling, "Ouch! Oww, stop!"

In the case of a child becoming overwhelmed and dysregulated, you can help them feel safe by saying something like "Hey, I know you don't want to talk about it, but if we don't talk about it now, then you'll be sad/worried/mad when it happens again, and I want to be able to help you! Can we talk about it for a little bit? Like two minutes? I'll set a timer!"

If the child continues to become dysregulated and upset despite your sincere efforts to keep them comfortable, you should back off and apologize. Then give the child space and offer them a blanket to hide behind, something to drink, or something to hold that will comfort them. Do not explain yourself further, as too many words will overstimulate them even more. Instead, go on to an engaging or soothing activity, such as The Weather Report, to help the child reset.

For the child who can tolerate talking, it is important to avoid pushing them to talk by saying something like "Come on, go ahead," or by touching them or staring at them. This doesn't serve connection. Sometimes you just have to experiment with a few responses until you land on one that resonates. For instance, I remember working with a 14-year-old girl who didn't want to be in residential treatment, didn't want to go to residential school, and just wanted to sit in the hallway. She felt like no one was listening to her, like no one was helping her. She wanted to go home, and she blamed everyone else and the staff for her frequent outbursts.

When I started working with her, she refused to talk. At first, I tried to empathize with how hard and lonely it was for her. I wanted to communicate that I understood and could listen to her hurt. She didn't like that at all; she refused to accept my empathy. I tried again. This time, I stopped and said, "Wait, so tell me what it is that you really want to tell me." She shouted, "I want you to send me home!" I then responded with strong vitality affect to match her own: "I really want to, and I know you're mad at me. I've disappointed you. Everyone here has. So has the whole system! I believe you! I am so sorry. But I can't send you home. I don't have a magic wand. I don't blame you if you are mad and disappointed."

I wanted to communicate to her that she was a survivor and that she had earned the right to not care and not cooperate. I wanted her to know that I knew that because people had disappointed her, she wanted to disappoint them—to not listen or care anymore. I wanted her to know that her feelings made sense. This, too, is an important kind of connection. While my words and affect didn't suddenly open her up to me, it was the beginning of more productive work.

In cases like this, you can determine if the child can tolerate hearing you say with urgency just how important it is that they talk: "I want you to talk because if we don't talk about it here, nobody will talk about it ever and it will keep happening. And you're alone with it! I don't want you to be alone with it!"

It isn't always so challenging, but coaxing a child to talk is a critical part of all therapy, including IAFT. Luckily, IAFT prioritizes tools for nonverbal communication, which enables you to establish a sense of safety and a kind of connection even when it cannot be verbally established. Think of it as connection through disconnection. Over time, these smaller connections can grow in strength and power, enabling regulation that fosters the safety the child requires to truly open up.

Fostering Deliberate Dialogue

Once you have established communication, it is time to engage in deliberate dialogue while prioritizing a PACEful attitude. For Whitney and Maya, communication was typically established through the preceding games or, if Maya didn't feel like participating in those, then through Maya's journal. After this connection was supported, Whitney and Maya shifted into deliberate dialogue, and the subject usually centered on Maya's refusal to go to school. As discussed in chapter 3, deliberate dialogue is structured with the following steps:

1. Connect and chat (this step is typically completed at the beginning of the session and need not be repeated)

2. Discuss and accept the difficulty

3. Empathize

4. Express curiosity

5. Wonder aloud

6. Get permission to guess

7. Guess

8. Validate and empathize

9. Connect to the past

10. Validate and empathize (again)

11. Facilitate the parent-child connection

12. Guide the parent to accept and empathize

13. Summarize and highlight positive attributes about the dyad

14. Problem solve

Here is how the IAFT therapist used these steps to foster a deliberate dialogue with Whitney and Maya.

1. Connect and Chat

As the therapist chatted with Maya, she noticed that Maya had cat hair on her sweater. When the therapist pointed this out, Maya animatedly explained that the neighborhood cat had kittens and that she loved to feed and hold them. Maya said she was a cat whisperer, and the therapist asked her to demonstrate. Maya then meowed in various ways to demonstrate how she spoke "cat." The therapist marveled at Maya's skills and asked if Maya could speak other animal languages, to which Maya said she could speak "turkey" as well. All three of them laughed, and then the therapist brought up the problem Whitney and Maya experienced yesterday morning.

2. Discuss and Accept the Difficulty

THERAPIST: So, you had a hard time yesterday morning because it was hard to get out of bed, and then you and Mom fought. There was yelling and stuff. Can you tell me more about that?

MAYA: I don't care about school! I don't learn anything important there. Mom says if I don't go to school, I won't go to university and get a good job, but I don't want to go to university anyway.

3. Empathize

THERAPIST: If you feel like school is boring and it's a waste of time and you don't learn anything important, no wonder you don't want to go.

4. Express Curiosity

THERAPIST [*in a true tone of curiosity*]: I wonder what they would teach at school that would feel important to you? Like what important things would you want to learn?

MAYA: Anything useful! Nothing they teach is relevant to me!

5. Wonder Aloud

THERAPIST [*avoiding looking directly at Maya*]: Hmm, I wonder why it's not relevant to you? [*Then, looking at Maya*] Do you know why?

MAYA: The teacher is dumb, and I don't plan to go to university anyway. I'm just going to work doing whatever.

6. Get Permission to Guess

THERAPIST: Okay, thanks for telling me that. I wonder if there's any other reason you don't want to go to school. Hmm . . . Hey, I've known some people in similar situations, so I wonder—can I guess why you don't care? Would that be okay?

MAYA: [*Shrugs.*]

THERAPIST: Okay, good, I'll guess.

7. Guess

THERAPIST [*posing questions rhetorically, wondering aloud about these guesses and looking to Maya for signs of nonverbal confirmation*]: Could it be that you feel kind of empty inside and that nothing interests you? Maybe you saw your mom work hard to study and if she is not working, you feel discouraged? Maybe you think you are somehow at fault for Mom losing her job? Or maybe you are afraid to try because you feel like you might fail no matter how hard you try?

8. Validate and Empathize (Again)

THERAPIST [*upon receiving Maya's confirmation that she fears she might fail no matter what*]: That makes sense! Of course you don't want to go to school if you feel like you might fail no matter how hard you try!

9. Connect to the Past

THERAPIST: Maybe it's because you have had a lot of fights at home, and you also feel like you failed to make things better and like the bad things that happen will never stop happening, so it's not worth trying?

10. Repeat with Empathy

THERAPIST [*upon receiving Maya's nonverbal confirmation*]: That makes even more sense! No wonder you don't want to go to school if you feel like it won't stop bad things from happening!

11. Facilitate the Parent-Child Connection

THERAPIST: Can you tell your mom how you felt? [*Maya shakes her head no.*] Can I talk for you? If I say anything wrong, you can let me know by telling me, but also, I'll look at you and notice. [*Maya nods her head yes, and the therapist moves closer to her side so she can talk for Maya from Maya's perspective.*] Mom, it's so hard for me to go to school in the morning. I worry that you're so stressed about me, and I want to go to school to make you feel better, but then I just lose hope that things will get better, and I can't face it.

12. Guide the Parent to Accept and Empathize

THERAPIST: Mom, can you say something accepting and empathic to let Maya know you can understand what it's like for her—something like "Thanks for telling me, Maya. That must have been scary if you think that not going to school is adding more stress for me. I can understand how that would make it even harder for you to get up and go to school if you feel so much pressure to make me feel better."

13. Summarize and Highlight Positive Attributes About the Dyad

THERAPIST [*talking in a melodic voice about the whole dialogue*]: Wow, Mom and Maya, I see some real strength in your relationship. You have had hard times, but you are talking here in a heart-to-heart way without hurting each other's feelings so much, and you didn't have to yell or run away. This is the beginning of something important between you two.

14. Problem Solve

THERAPIST: Maya, Whitney, do you have a sense of what makes it better or less stressful in the morning? All three of us are smart, and I bet we can brainstorm together.

MAYA: If you just don't act so incredibly intense in the morning.

WHITNEY: I can try, but you still need to go to school.

THERAPIST: Whitney, I think it's worth focusing on coming in and waking Maya up with less intensity. Part of the stress of the situation is the stress of your relationship, so by being more accepting in the morning, I think Maya will appreciate that. But, if there are some days that Maya can't get out of bed, you may have to accept that. Perhaps she can go for a half a day instead of a whole day.

MAYA: I guess I can try to go for a half a day if I feel better.

WHITNEY: Okay, I can try not to be so pushy in the morning.

MAYA: Thanks, Mom.

Once the deliberate dialogue concludes, the session shifts to another, shorter period of play. This helps to reestablish connection and conclude the session. Often this playtime makes use of touch, a critical component of regulation and connection. When they were able to tolerate it, Whitney and Maya particularly liked to play Weather Report, bringing the session to a close with a gentle, calming touch. They also liked pretending to use their fingers as tattoo pens, drawing (and narrating) pictures on each other's backs.

Reflection

Whitney and Maya had so much stress in the relationship due to Whitney's childhood, marital trauma, and depression. Having just emerged from a bad marriage, Whitney wanted Maya to be functional and healthy, and she wanted her to simply press forward with life and school. When Maya showed symptoms of depression, anxiety, and school refusal, Whitney was impatient and reactive, feeling as though she was at fault. She also felt resentful, as though Maya didn't appreciate all that Whitney did for her.

When they began therapy, they had not experienced fun and connection for a long time. As therapy continued, the process of playing helped Whitney and Maya connect on a joyful, physical level. In fact, one time, when Maya blew a feather toward her mom's face and Whitney caught it on the tip of her tongue, they both laughed so hard they almost began to cry. When they calmed down, they reflected on how they couldn't remember the last time they had laughed like that together. The activities that involved touch were also calming and connecting. Whitney learned to touch Maya in ways that were pleasant when they were not fighting, and that made it easier to reach out and offer comfort to Maya when she was stressed in the morning.

As Whitney participated in parent-only sessions, she was increasingly able to identify her own feelings of worry and fear and to become less reactive. Through attachment work and guided meditation, she was able to listen to some of the negative criticisms in her head and realize they were coming from her own self, that she was her own worst persecutor. Whitney was able to come to terms with and process her own feelings of fear and self-blame, and she was able to find some compassion for herself. She was also able to accept that she could not control Maya's behavior in the ways she had been trying to thus far.

During dyadic sessions, Whitney was more capable of listening to Maya's fears and hesitations about school. Maya was able to communicate that she was sometimes worried about disappointing Whitney and that, at other times, she wanted to stay home to make sure Whitney was okay. Although this was very hard for Whitney to hear, it was important that she was able to validate those feelings without dismissing or justifying them. Ultimately, Whitney increasingly used the PACE attitude at home, which reduced their blow-ups. Whitney was also able to accept that Maya needed a modified school schedule, and eventually Maya went to an alternative school for half a year.

In the context of the multifaceted process of IAFT, the dyadic sessions combine all the elements in the course of care, including the parent intake and attachment history, the connective play and deliberate dialogue, and the continuous parent work to help foster and strengthen a sense of safety and connection. For Whitney and Maya, these elements helped make their mother-daughter relationship less caustic and more productive. Maya was able to use Whitney as a resource rather than see her as someone to avoid. Because Whitney became less defensive and calmer, Whitney was able to see what Maya really needed, which was support for her anxiety at school through special services.

9

Common Challenges to Implementing IAFT

IAFT is incredibly effective at fostering and strengthening safety and connection. However, as with any framework, therapists may face a variety of challenges in implementing it. Typically, such challenges fall into three categories:

- Challenges for the therapist

- Challenges for the parent

- Challenges for the child

Each of these categories poses a challenge to the therapist because they can lead to dysregulation, stuck points, or inefficacy. Knowing more about these challenges—how, when, and why they pop up—can go a long way toward preparing you to respond effectively during sessions.

Common Challenges for the Therapist

By this point, you have probably come up against or considered your own personal challenges to implementing IAFT. Some therapists feel a sense of overwhelm about its process, while others feel unsure how to implement their new knowledge of polyvagal theory and the varieties of nonverbal communication. Others may feel wary about inviting parents into the process in a fundamental way. However, the most common challenge for an IAFT therapist is usually the feeling of uncertainty that can arise during sessions. At any point during any session, you may suddenly feel that the next steps are unclear, that you are lost, and that your mind is blank. You may wonder if you've gone deep enough, if you've gotten to a meaningful core issue, or if you will trigger or dysregulate the child (and retraumatize them) if you go deeper. At those moments, you aren't sure what to do.

Of course, uncertainty is part of the implementation of any new framework. This is why I recommend practicing the exercises described in the previous chapters, such as mapping your autonomic ladder, understanding and using the PACE attitude, practicing the SES activities, and engaging in self-guided meditation. It's not that practicing these tools and techniques will lessen your doubts, fears, or panic, it's that practicing them will prepare you for their certain arrival. The fact is, feeling doubt, feeling panic, or simply drawing a blank during a session are all part of the process. As the PACE attitude teaches you, the first and most important thing you can do is practice acceptance. When you can accept that your doubts, fears, and panic are constitutive to the process, you can reduce the sense of emergency associated with your panic, just a bit.

Once you've accepted the part played by doubt, fear, and panic, you can prepare for their arrival in sessions. Try to notice who and what triggers your autonomic nervous system response. For example, you might feel that certain clients or certain situations provoke a fire in your stomach, or you might recognize your own fight-or-flight response. When you begin to sense these feelings, anchor yourself with deep breathing. Guide yourself through the same meditation exercises you use with clients.

During sessions, as you begin to feel doubt, fear, or panic, you might also consider externalizing your experience by speaking out loud to your client. You might say something like "Hey, hold on a minute. You said something important, and then you hid under the blanket, and now I'm thinking, *Hey, what's going on here?* I don't know what to say or in which direction to go. I need to think about this for a minute." Then, importantly, allow yourself to think! Allow yourself to listen for what your client is really saying. Listen for the music of their words—and imagine what they are saying underneath those words and behind those behaviors.

It can be useful to put stickers in a couple corners of the room, near the top of the wall, so you can use these as a focal point while you reflect. As you continue to repeat this reflective posture, your clients will learn that this is your thinking posture, and they will accept and respect it. In general, I find that when you are sincere and transparent with clients about your uncertainty about what to do next, clients will wait with you, silently supporting you as they allow you time to think.

I also want to note here that the dual experience is real. What do I mean by "the dual experience"? This occurs when, in session, you feel divided between your external presentation—in which your SES is fully online, and you have vitality in your voice, movement in your face, good voice prosody, and loose gestures—and your internal experience, which may feel full of doubt, fear, or even panic. This division may make you feel like a fake or a phony. Or it may make you feel like a robot. Or you may hear an internal voice screaming, *You're in danger!* or *This isn't going to work!* This, too, is normal. The dual experience is the result of your monitoring both your internal and external experiences. In session, you are guiding your mind to do the behaviors that you know will help your client, even though on the inside these behaviors may make you feel uncomfortable. As with any new method, the gap between these experiences will become smaller the more you practice and the more evidence you gather about the method's success.

Common Challenges for the Parent

Parents face a variety of challenges when acclimating to IAFT. Many of these challenges pose obstacles for the therapist too.

Monologues

Many parents arrive to IAFT sessions with pent-up feelings, concerns, and complaints that they want to get off their chests. Sometimes, these parents fall into the habit of delivering lengthy monologues during sessions, both parent-only and dyadic. A monologue can make you feel like your client is barraging you with words. It may feel as though they are rushing at you like a torrential river, flooding you with facts, feelings, and stories. This can be exhausting, and you may begin to feel weak, tired, resentful, unheard, or bulldozed.

In these moments, it is useful to increase your vitality affect to amplify the energy in the room. This can involve increasing your physical presence through movement: flapping your hands, waving your arms, using your voice, and getting back to the rhythm of talking. It can also mean interjecting. You may want to say something like "Wait, wait, wait, I have to tell you something. The reason I interrupted you is _____. This is what I want to focus on." It is important at these times to act as an interventionist. You can certainly apologize for the interruption, but you also want to explain to the parent that it is best to slow down, focus, and deal with one thing at a time. This is important for a variety of reasons, but primarily it is necessary to ensure their nervous system remains calm and regulated, which, in turn, enables you to offer real help.

The most straightforward way to use your vitality to stop a parent from monologuing requires you to express a lot of energy and be actively present. This can mean nodding, rocking, offering a lot of verbal agreement, using your hands to gesture, or using the time-out sign with them. It is best to use these from the very beginning of your sessions together. By beginning these interactions early, you will help the parent acclimate to your strong, regulating presence. If, on the other hand, you wait quietly and politely for them to finish their sentences, then a parent who is already meandering, dysregulated, and unfocused may get used to a dynamic in which they frequently flood you—and potentially their child, in dyadic sessions—with monologues, and it will be harder to intervene and regulate them.

Minor Stuck Points*

During IAFT, a parent will usually reach one or more stuck points. Sometimes these are big and hard to move past, in which case the parent will benefit from a guided meditation in a parent-only session, as discussed in chapter 7. However, parents will often stumble across smaller stuck points as well. These minor stuck points are usually a sign that the parent is grappling with their own fear, hurt, rage, or sadness.

When a parent reaches this kind of stuck point, it's not helpful to offer psychoeducation about the child's development or about trauma responses, or to recommend yet another book to read or technique to try. In these moments, the parent is in pain; they need to feel heard and to feel that their feelings are accepted and validated. Without this, the parent will not be able to become aware of how the feelings that are causing them to feel stuck are the same feelings that are impacting and influencing their behavior toward their child.

Just as you respond to a dysregulated child, when you recognize that a parent is at a stuck point, it is critical to listen—to really listen empathically—using the PACE attitude. You can focus on making your empathic response come to life, showing the parent that you believe them and are really *with* them by using SES techniques (including voice prosody and resonance, facial expressions and eye contact, and touch, gestures, and posture) to nonverbally communicate that you understand.

---

* This material is adapted from chapter 21 in Norris and Lender (2020).

It is usually obvious when a parent reaches a stuck point because they signal it through a number of common statements. Let's take a look at some common stuck point statements, the possible feelings and beliefs underlying those stuck points, and helpful responses.

Parent statement: "My child just needs to listen to/respect me as the parent."

Potential feelings:

- The parent may feel insulted by their child's disregard.
- The parent may feel a form of latent rage associated with having been shamed or humiliated as a child.
- They may feel that their family or society is blaming them.
- They may feel like a failure.
- They may feel out of control or may fear that their child will be hurt.
- They may feel they are being rejected by their child and feel the associated pain of rejection.

Potential response: For a parent who is struggling with feeling that their child just needs to listen to or respect them, it is important to help the parent grapple with the reality that they do not have control over another person. They only have control over themselves. It is also necessary to provide the parent with emotional support and to direct them toward self-care.

Parent statement: "I was raised this way, and I turned out okay."

Potential feelings:

- The parent may be worried that something is, in fact, wrong with them and that this is the reason for their problems with their child.
- They may feel reluctant to consider or examine whether they really did turn out okay.

Potential response: It is important to communicate that you hear and can validate the parent's feelings. First, show the parent that you can see their good intentions. For example: "Thanks for telling me. The way you have been raised and the way you have been operating has made you the person you are today. You are a strong person. You have learned to get things done and soldier on in the face of adversity. I think that's really admirable. I'm guessing that's what you want for your child too—you want to give them a leg up in this world by instilling this value in them."

Next, indicate that you understand the feeling that might be buried underneath their claim that everything is okay: "Here's my concern—I'm worried that there is a price you had to pay for that upbringing. It seems as though you might have paid a price, like feeling lonely or not lovable? Or finding relationships difficult? You're hard on yourself, and if there is conflict, you retreat. I'm wondering if your child may need something different."

Parent statement: "Are you saying I should just let my child do that?"

Potential feelings:

- The parent may feel a sense of hopelessness, as though this is how it's always going to be and they'll have to live in this painful moment forever.

- The parent may feel a lack of control, which can feel upsetting or even terrifying.

Potential response: It is important to communicate to the parent that you do not agree with their child's behavior but that the behavior can lead the way to the underlying issue. Parents typically feel vulnerable in these moments, even if their words are said with anger or some aggression. The parent may feel as though you're siding with the child by allowing the child's behavior. Consequently, you want to emphasize that although you do not think the child's behavior is problem-free, it can help you uncover the source of the problem.

For example: "Oh, I apologize. I don't think it's okay for your child to mistreat you. Part of what I think is going on for them when they get into that mode is that they experience a kind of an explosion, and they aren't actually aware of their response. Thanks so much for telling me about your concern. I hear your desperation and am going to be working on that with you. At the same time, if we can't figure out what the underlying issue is, we are going to be doing the same thing over and over again."

Parent statement: "Why am I the one who has to do all the changing?"

Potential feelings:

- The parent may feel completely exhausted, as though they've been climbing this mountain for too long and can't go any farther.

- They may feel resentful, as though they've been trying all along and have not only not been recognized for their efforts but now have to work harder and change more.

Potential response: When a parent expresses this kind of stuck point, it's important to communicate to them that they are in control and that they can make choices that will help alleviate them of the burden they may be feeling in trying to change their relationship with their child. You might say: "You don't have to change if you don't want to. I certainly hear where you are coming from. You're the one who's been doing this for so long, and you're the one who is being asked to change. That must be exhausting. Is there anything that could help take the burden off you so that you could make more space for your own feelings and needs?"

Once you've offered the parent a PACEful response, brainstorm options with them that might lead to relief. Such options could include asking for help from their spouse or friends, or finding ways to integrate more self-care into their days.

Parent statement: "How will playing help?"

Potential feelings:

- The parent may not have been played with as a child or may not have relevant experiences to drawn on.

- They may not associate play with positivity and may not understand that play can result in positive change.

- They may fear that you are not taking their worries and concerns seriously or that play is not a real treatment.

- They may feel that you don't understand the gravity of their situation and that play is a directionless pursuit.

- The parent may be so hurt that they want the child to feel the consequences of the pain that the parent feels within the parent-child relationship.

> **Potential response:** For this parent, it is important to explore their potential feelings with curiosity. It may be useful or necessary to talk through the possible feelings associated with this statement to find out which one most resonates with the parent. Then, it is critical to demonstrate acceptance of their feelings and provide empathy for the experiences that contributed to those feelings. At this point, it may also be useful to reframe the utility of play too.

Redirection

In both parent-only and dyadic sessions, parents may get lost in their own monologues or run into their own stuck points. It's easy to recognize the need for redirection because it typically presents as a parent's rant, as spiraling negativity, or with a flooding of the therapist or any other family members in the session. To guide the parent back to more productive work, follow the three Ps:

1. Pause

2. Prep

3. Pivot

This is an intervention for taking back the lead in a session. It is especially useful when a parent is dysregulated and ranting, spiraling, or flooding. You can use this in a dyadic session when you need to interrupt either the parent or the child and refocus them. You can also use it in an individual session, and it can be especially useful during parent-only meetings.

The three Ps are relatively straightforward: *Pause* refers to the pause you insert by interrupting or slowing down a parent who is swept away by their own narrative and who is no longer in productive conversation with you, their child, or the other parent. *Prep* is the space you create for the parent to gather themselves for a moment of re-regulation. *Pivot* is the direction you take the parent, and the session, after the pause and prep.

Let's take a closer look at the process. Many times, in parent-only sessions, parents feel stressed and desperate to get answers. They may railroad you with example after example or complaint after complaint. You may try to help them by answering their questions or by providing some education around their complaints, but they can't take in what you're saying to them; they can't even hear you. At this point, the three Ps can help regulate and focus them:

Pause: A pause helps a parent who is flooding you with information or escalating their nonverbal and verbal communications. For this parent, it can be useful to interrupt them or slow them down.

Pause statements:

- "Hey, can I slow you down?"
- "Can we slow down for a moment?"
- "Can we have a time-out?" [Make a T with your hands.]
- "Can we press the pause button?" [Make a pressing-down motion with your hand flat.]

Because you are pausing a parent in the midst of a dysregulated moment, it is likely that you will have to increase your vitality affect by, for example, using resonance and making big gestures in order to reach them.

Prep: Prep helps a parent who is feeling emotionally activated and who needs time to shift states, calm down, and re-regulate. They need time to "get it back together," and they then need to be prepared to change their state of mind.

Prep statements: Before offering a prep statement, take a moment to take a deep, dramatic breath. This signals to the parent that you and the parent are now shifting states. It also signals that the parent can and should participate in the deep, dramatic breath, and this helps to re-regulate them. Next, say:

- "Can I give you a heads up?"
- "I need to give you a heads up."
- "I'm going to tell you something that's a little difficult to hear. Are you ready for it?"

Give the parent a few moments to shift their stance or point of view. As you give them this time, signal that you are also ready for the shift by taking deep, regulated breaths.

If they are not able to calm themselves in advance of the shift—if they show that they are upset by continuing to talk, flailing their arms, pacing, or otherwise acting agitated—change the course of the session. Do this by getting up to get the parent a glass of water, by suggesting that you both take a walk outside, by suggesting that they go to the bathroom and splash water on their face, or by suggesting that they think about the most comfortable ways they can calm down or take care of themselves in the moment. If this happens during a dyadic session, you might have to end the session by separating the dyad and working with the parent while the child waits in the waiting room.

Pivot: A pivot helps to redirect a parent or a session. It consists of a clear, short, directive statement about where the session needs to go, or what your main point is: What, in this moment, do you really need the client to hear?

Pivot statements:

- "I'm trying to teach you a new way of interacting that's different from what you do at home."

- "I am asking you to focus less on behavior and more on what your child is feeling underneath."

The three Ps process enables you to redirect and refocus the parent in the more regulated and productive direction that you would like the session to go. It also reassures the parent that you are a leader. The parent may bristle in the moment, but underneath, they will most likely feel reassured that you not only see their need but are comfortably in control of responding to it on more productive terms.

Reorganize Hopelessness

Occasionally, a depressed parent can become more despairing even as you offer interventions. For instance, when offering PACEful responses to a depressed parent, the parent may become even more upset. The very acceptance and empathy you want to give the parent seems to make them go deeper into hopelessness. You may feel that you're reenforcing depression and despair.

In these cases, acceptance and empathy are still important, but you may need to shift out of simple validation and instead use vitality affect and your SES capacities to communicate that you understand just how hard, sad, or painful the parent's life is. This is often difficult because it requires you to shift the session with an energetic intervention, thereby increasing hopefulness and, potentially, a sense of progress. To do this effectively, consider the following strategy:

1. First, check in with yourself. If you are feeling sad because of the empathy you are offering through PACE, your face and body are likely reflecting sadness or hopelessness. Take a moment to demonstrate, in your body, a shift toward energetic openness. You may need to shake your shoulders, take a breath, or unfurrow your brow.

2. Next, give the parent context, and show them support and encouragement. Consider communicating something like this: "The reason you feel so hopeless is because your situation is super difficult; anyone would feel this way. You're a good person in a difficult situation. There is no magic solution. What we need to do is make you feel as supported as you can. It's not your fault, and you have value. If your child does something bad, it's not because of you. I admire you. Can you take care of yourself and find more support around you?"

3. Then, offer statements to pivot to a more strength-based perspective: "Okay, you've been in really hard situations before—tell me about a time when things seemed hopeless but you resolved the problem."

4. If the parent can't think of an example, but you can think of one from your previous sessions, bring the previous session to their attention.

5. Next, ask them to identify another moment when they felt similarly hopeless: "Where else have you felt this kind of hopelessness in your life—when you couldn't do anything, or when you felt particularly ineffective?"

6. Finally, explain that this moment—today—is different from the moment from the past: "I want you to separate that past time from today. Today, you can try out something new, just as an experiment."

If, as you work with the parent, they imply that they are thinking about doing something drastic, you should explicitly name this implicit thought and ask about it. For parents, as well as for children and others, it can be a relief when someone guesses their dark thoughts and normalizes them. "Something drastic" in this context might mean asking a parent who feels hopeless about their foster child if they are thinking of ending placement. This thought, from the parent's perspective, is often deeply shameful, and it is important to explain to the parent in this moment that you're not judging them. For another parent, "something drastic" might mean suicidal ideation, so you would want to ask, "Are you thinking about suicide?" In this case, it is necessary to inquire into these thoughts, to conduct a formal risk assessment, and, if warranted, to develop a safety plan.

Managing a Parent Who Interrupts

Although the preceding sections speak (generally) to parent-only sessions, parents can pose challenges in dyadic sessions as well. The most common challenge they pose in these sessions is a tendency to interrupt.

Parents often interrupt when they want to defend or explain themselves. For instance, when the child describes the challenges they're experiencing from their own perspective, the parent often tries to jump in to provide what they see as a corrective solution. In this situation, it is necessary to tell the parent that it's important to hear what is on the child's mind. Remind them that you are listening for the music underneath the words. Reassure them that they will have an opportunity to articulate their perspective later.

Since this is more easily illustrated through an example, let's return to Whitney and Maya, whom you may recall from the previous chapter. While Whitney and Maya were able to reach a variety of relationship goals over the course of therapy, during the middle phases of the work, their dyadic sessions were characterized by Whitney's frequent interruptions. As is common, Whitney interrupted in order to defend and explain herself. While her desire to interrupt was understandable— she often expressed feeling blamed for her relationship problems with Maya, and she often presented as dysregulated—the interruptions posed a challenge for productive therapy. The conversation that follows is an excerpt from the middle of one of their dyadic sessions, and it offers strategies for getting a parent like Whitney back on track.

> THERAPIST: All right. So, Maya, I know you had a tough week. As we discussed, you woke up and didn't feel well on Wednesday. And you and your mom went around and around about going to school. You argued

about whether you had to go to school that day or if you could take a mental health day. Your mom said that you already took a few mental health days and couldn't take any more. Can you recall how you were feeling that morning? I'm really interested in how you felt as you were waking up. How did you feel, Maya? Do you remember?

MAYA: Yeah. Like, I felt like shit, like how I feel every day, like there was no change. I woke up and I was like, what's the point? What's the point of going to school? And, like, even trying, there's no point.

WHITNEY [*interrupting in an exasperated, sarcastic tone*]: Wow! Well, yes, there is a point to going to school. It's because you need to get your education so that you can do what you need to do in life.

THERAPIST: Hey, Whitney, wait a second. I have to tell you something. What we need to do is to first really check in with Maya about her experience and her fears. If you give her a rational explanation, it's going to shut her down, at least for now. Right now, we have to just listen to where she's at, and then we'll go from there. Is that okay? Can you hang in there with me?

WHITNEY: I mean, I guess it's just that, you know, when I was growing up, I just had to—

THERAPIST [*interrupting Whitney*]: Go to school. I know. Hold on a second. You're worried. Yep. You know what? You're super worried. I hear you about this. What I want to preserve here is the possibility of talking about this in a different way than how you talk about it at home. And so, you've got to work with me on this part to see if we can do it differently here and get to a little bit of a different result. Is that something that you can work with me on?

WHITNEY: [*Nods.*]

THERAPIST: Okay. So, for now, I'm going to find out from Maya, and then I promise you'll get a chance to have your say.

WHITNEY: [*Nods in agreement.*]

THERAPIST [*turning to Maya*]: Maya, you were saying you feel like shit every day?

MAYA: Yeah. For a really long time. Like I just don't belong anywhere.

THERAPIST: You don't belong anywhere. When did that start? You said you've been feeling it for a really long time, feeling like you don't belong anywhere. Do you remember when this feeling first started? Or, to think about it a little differently, do you remember ever feeling like you had a sense of belonging anywhere?

MAYA: I don't know. A while ago, at school, I was pretending to be with the cool crowd, I guess, but then things were so messed up at home, and I felt weird about it. I just stopped going to school 'cause I was feeling really low. Then one day, I started, you know, just wanting to be in my bed all the time. And my mom just doesn't help. She just tells me, like, things I should be doing. And when I feel so low, it doesn't really help.

THERAPIST: Okay. So, you said something important there—

WHITNEY: [*Sighs loudly, overtly rolling her eyes.*]

THERAPIST [*to Whitney*]: Wait, hold on. Wait. I know. Whitney, your daughter said something incredibly important, and I really want us to listen because I think we're onto something here. I really want us to hear what she said about school, so hang in here with me.

WHITNEY: [*Straightens up, tries to gain composure, and nods her head a little.*]

THERAPIST [*to Maya*]: Okay, Maya, you said you were pretending, right? Is that what you said before? That you were having to pretend that your family was okay in order to fit in?

MAYA: [*Nods.*]

THERAPIST: Right. Yeah.

WHITNEY [*interrupting the silence*]: Yeah, Maya? Like, every family has burdens in life? They're not always happy. Our family is not perfect, but we are pretty good.

THERAPIST: Oh gosh, hold on a second. Maya, can you hold on just a second?

MAYA: [*Nods warily.*]

THERAPIST [*turns to Whitney*]: Hey, Whitney, I'm worried. I'm a little worried that Maya is actually speaking from her heart, and I think we're getting to the bottom of something right now, but I also feel like you're feeling upset because you think I'm criticizing you or something like that? And I know this is all very painful to hear. I know your daughter is talking about some really hard things, right? But I think that this is the core of some of the conflicts between you two. So I really need to check in with you. Do you feel like you can maybe take some pressure off yourself right now? I'm not blaming you, and I'm not going to leave you alone or out of it, but I wonder if you are able to do this right now? Would you like to get some water? Do you want to grab something that you can hold on to, like a little loving object? Or can you put your hand on your heart to give yourself some source of comfort as you listen? What do you think, Whitney? I'm asking you.

WHITNEY [*swallowing, trying to gain composure*]: I could probably use something to drink.

THERAPIST [*hands Whitney water, and Whitney drinks*]: Okay, good. Would you hold that? And would you also just take yourself off the hook for a minute? I don't want you to feel like I'm blaming you. Okay? But I know you're eager to connect with your daughter and she's telling us some really important things. I know you're really trying, and I appreciate it.

THERAPIST [*turns back to Maya*]: All right, Maya. You were saying that part of you felt that in order to fit in, you had to pretend like your family was okay—but you weren't okay. And maybe you thought that the other kids' families were okay and different in a better way?

MAYA: I think I would sit in class and just worry about going home because, you know, I didn't know if it was going to be safe, or if Mom was going to be safe, or if she was even going to be, like, out of bed some days. And it's just . . . that's all I was thinking about.

THERAPIST: Okay, good. Well, you know what? This is incredibly courageous of you and super, super smart. You were so courageous to be able to be aware of what you were experiencing back then, because this was a while back already. At the time, you were scared. And today you still remember feeling like you did in the classroom, worried about what was happening at home. Okay, now I'm going to turn to your mom for a second. I'm going to check in with her.

MAYA: [*Nods.*]

THERAPIST [*turning to Whitney*]: Hey, Whitney, what do you think? I think I can see that part of you wants to reassure Maya and say that, although it may have been that way in the past, it isn't the same now. But part of you is also able to really hear and understand her. I can see it in your eyes. Would you be willing to respond if she told you about her feelings directly and talked to you about them? Would you be able to tell her that you can understand? That you can understand how she might have had those worries back then and that they might still come up for her now? Can you say something accepting and something empathic like we practiced?

WHITNEY: Maya, I appreciate that you are wanting to figure this out. You're wanting to figure out how to go to school and what that's going to look like. And you're wondering whether or not I'm going to be helpful in those moments because in the past, I wasn't helpful. I'm really sorry that I made you feel that way. And, you know, it's just definitely been hard for all of us and that, um, you know, I have things that I need to accomplish, too, and I just need you to get up and go to school because—

THERAPIST [*to Whitney*]: Let's just focus on acceptance and empathy. You can say something along the lines of "Thanks for telling me that."

WHITNEY: Thanks for telling me that you were worried about the family and that you felt weird about what was happening at home.

THERAPIST: That's great, Whitney! Can you say something empathic, too? About, for instance, how it would be hard to concentrate in school if you felt weird and uncomfortable and worried?

WHITNEY: Yeah. That would be really hard if you felt so bad and weird about what was happening at home. And you were worried about me.

THERAPIST: That's really great, Whitney. And Maya, you are being very courageous.

In this session, it's clear that Whitney wanted to defend herself. But when she did so, she repeated the patterns that she and Maya were stuck in. Instead, the therapist addressed Whitney every time she interrupted, reminding her of the goal of the conversation, reassuring her that she would have time to discuss her own feelings, and supporting her through offering a PACEful attitude. Each parent's interruptions may take a slightly different form, but they can all be handled in a similar way.

Common Challenges for the Child

Child-related challenges are such a standard part of dyadic sessions that I hesitate to include them in their own separate section. However, some children— notably those who do not seem to want to participate in play or who have been categorized as "withdrawn," "hyperactive," or "uncooperative"—benefit from the play repertoires that follow. Most of these activities come from the Theraplay activities canon, a complete list of which can be found in *Theraplay: The Practitioner's Guide* (Norris & Lender, 2020). These noncompetitive games can provide 15 to 20 minutes of cooperative play to create moments of fun, joy, and connection between parent and child in the first part of the dyadic session. However, not every child requires these play repertoires, and some children will benefit from different approaches to play regardless of their particular profile.

To determine an appropriate repertoire for a child who does not want to participate in play, it's necessary to figure out *why* the child does not want to participate. If, for instance, the child is withdrawn or passive, they may be in a dorsal vagal mode because they are hurt and traumatized, and they have therefore contracted into themselves for self-protection. Or they may be withdrawn or passive because they have figured out that acting this way can activate their parent into a certain type of reaction—such as giving in to their demands, doing things for them, or expressing irritation at them. It is also possible to have a mixture of these two (or other) underlying motives, but the more dominant theme will typically determine your approach.

If you face difficulty, or if you chose one approach and it fails, do not fret. You can simply see your chosen approach as an experiment that needs to be adjusted or tweaked for improved results. Rest assured, you have not traumatized the child or failed at being a playful therapist. The most important thing is that you show the child that you are genuinely interested in playing with them, delighting in them, and getting to know them, and that if they reject you, you do not react with hurt, defensiveness, or discouragement. The child needs to feel that even if they are pushing you away, not cooperating, or acting chaotically, you still care about them and think they are an interesting and worthwhile play partner.

For the Withdrawn or Passive Child

This child typically benefits from activities that do not require overt cooperation, such as the following.

THE LOOKING GAME

Tell the child to look somewhere in the room, then you and the parent try to guess what the child is looking at. Ask the child to blink twice quickly if you guess right. Take turns as the looker. It's okay if the child is unwilling to vocalize or actively take part when it is the parent's or therapist's turn to be the looker.

STICK OUT ONE FOOT

If the child looks frozen or withdrawn, give them pillows and blankets to hide under, as this can go a long way toward making the child feel safer and more relaxed. Next, tell the child to stick out one foot. Express admiration for their foot or shoe to let the child know you really care and take genuine interest in them. Then play games just with that foot: Pretend the foot is a head and have the foot wiggle side to side for no, and up and down for yes. Ask the foot to answer yes/no questions such as "Foot, do you like chocolate ice cream?" You can also make a print of the bottom of their shoe (or foot) by wrapping aluminum foil around their shoe and then showing it to them. You can then ask them to stick out a knee, elbow, or hand and play the same game.

FEATHER DARTBOARD

For this game, described in the previous chapter, the parent can use a handful of feathers and try to blow them onto a specific target on the child. This game is easy and fun, and it requires little activity on the part of the child.

For the Hyperactive Child

A child who is running around the room, switching quickly from activity to activity, or trying to rummage through your supplies is a child who needs regulation. It is easy to see that this child is in a sympathetic nervous system state. Start regulating by matching their energy and joining in their behavior in some way, but also organizing their bodily movements as you join them. Activities that alternate between stopping and starting, or between slow and fast movements, will help harness the child's energy and shift it from chaotic to flowing and cooperative. Here are some activities to try.

THE JUMPING GAME

If a child is jumping or climbing on the couch, harness that behavior by holding their hands and saying, "Oh, you are an excellent jumper! I want to see if you can jump three times on the couch holding my hands, and then jump to the ground!" For this game and others like it, it is important to remember that you are in charge of the safety in the room. You can say that out loud to the child, but it is something you must also show in your actions. You must make sure that neither the child nor the parent is in the way or at risk of getting hurt if the child jumps from the couch. If someone does get hurt, you must take responsibility for not maintaining safety.

ATLAS GAME

Have the child stand with their arms above their head and their elbows bent, and then place a pillow on their hands. Position the parent in front of the child, facing them. Then, you or the parent says, "1, 2, 3, Atlas!" and the child lets the pillow drop into the parent's arms. Repeat by stacking two pillows at a time, then three pillows, then more. Admire the child's strength and balance each time. Consider alternating this same game with the child's legs and feet. In this case, the child lies on the ground with their feet in the air, and the parent is positioned in front of their legs. Place the pillows one by one to see how many you can stack before tumbling them into the parent's arms.

THE GIANT AWAKENS

Prepare for this game by having the child lie in the fetal position on the floor. Place pillows and blankets on top of the child (be sure they are comfortable and can breathe easily). Once they are covered, start the game. You and the parent walk around the room, saying:

> Sleeping giant in the night,
> don't come out until there's light.
>
> Sleeping giant, light of day,
> please wake up—it's time to play.

Repeat this while circling the child until the child pops out from underneath the pillows. Greet the child and marvel at their strength. Feel their arm and leg muscles and admire how capable they are.

THE SHAKES

This game is done standing up. You, the parent, and the child join hands, interlacing your fingers. Then shake your hands at the wrists and say:

> I got the shakes in my hands, and I don't know what they're doing!
> I don't know where they're going next!

Oh no! They're moving! Where are they moving? To my arms!

[*Flap your arms and continue*]:

I got the shakes in my arms, and I don't know what they're doing!
I don't know where they're going next! . . .

Repeat and shake all the different parts of your body. At the end, send the shakes back into your hands and say: "Let's get rid of these shakes! On the count of three, let's jump in the air really high. One, two, three!" Jump up with your hands in the air like you're throwing a basketball. Then put your arms at your side and hold still. Ask, "Did we get rid of the shakes?!" If the child's body is still, say, "Yes, we did!" If the child's body is active, repeat. The child and parent can also take turns being the leader.

SOCK GRAB

You (or the parent) and the child sit on the floor with your legs extended and the bottoms of your feet nearly touching. Each person removes one sock completely and pulls the other sock off the end of the foot just a bit. (Athletic tube socks work great for this game.) On the cue of "Ready, steady, go!" each player tries to grab the opponent's sock off their foot using only their toes while at the same time trying to keep their own sock from being grabbed and pulled off.

HEAVY WORK

This is an activity that occupational therapists use to calm active children. Heavy work requires a child to focus on using their strength to lift, move, or carry something heavy. This provides the child's joints and tendons with a lot of stimulation, enabling them to understand, with and through their bodies, where they are in space. This kind of bodily stimulation is called proprioception, and it can help their bodies feel calm.

For the Uncooperative Child

Children who are oppositional or controlling are often filled with shame. Many times, they have the self-image that they are bad, so they manifest this behavior of being uncooperative and negative so as to at least feel a little control about when and how that sense of badness will be shown. These are children who are also very sensitive to making mistakes and being called out or embarrassed. With these children, any activity can trigger their shame, so rather than thinking about ideal activities, it's better to focus more on how to respond to their needs:

- **Do not interpret oppositionality as anger, disregard, or disrespect.** For example, you might be playing a simple basketball game by throwing a wadded-up piece of paper into the wastebasket. The child might complain that the basket is too close and that it's too easy. But when you move the basket farther away and they miss, they get upset and take the other wadded-up pieces of paper and throw them around the room. In this case, you could say, "Wow, that was a good shot. It didn't work. Let's take another shot when you're ready." They will fuss and kick, and maybe move away from you. This is their shame reaction. At this point, it is best not to talk a lot. Perhaps distract them with a sip of ice water from a straw. Or perhaps they want to hide in a fort of pillows for a minute. After a minute or two has passed, invite them back into the next activity.

- **Do not engage, consciously or unconsciously, in a power struggle.** If they argue, pout, refuse to play, or disrupt the game for others, it is best not to confront this child by insisting they follow the rules. Playful teasing, like saying, "Oh, you're a sneaky devil!" can also provoke and incite more defiance or oppositionality.

To avoid power struggles, it's best to play games with flexible rules. Of course, in reality, many children's games have rules about right and wrong, and winners and losers. Usually, parents and other family members already have a set pattern in place of one or two predictable reactions. They will reason, negotiate, tease, and then get frustrated or show exasperation. Instead, when the child argues, pouts, refuses to play, or disrupts the game for others, you have a couple of options for moving forward.

First, you can wrap up the activity matter-of-factly but without reprimand and without showing disappointment with the child. Your behavior and attitude are the most important factor at this time because you are leading the child and the parent. Show the child that they have not disrupted your equilibrium or your positive regard for them. Simply offer a new game. You do not have to cajole, engage, or convince the child, or explain what has just happened and why you stopped playing the game. The child knows very well what happened—their parents have already explained it to them many times—and likely feels sensitive and defensive. At this moment, the child (like anyone, including adults) does not want to hear another person's voice; that would be overstimulating and would perpetuate the sympathetic nervous system response. They also don't want to hear reasons and rationales. They have heard them before and do not know why they can't control themselves.

Second, you can let the child take a break, perhaps with pillows to hug or to hide under, and drink some water so they can re-regulate for a minute or two. The feeling of shame is strong and needs to dissipate. If you gauge that, after a minute or two, the child is receptive, try initiating a deliberate dialogue. You can do this without requiring a direct response from the child. In fact, if appropriate, you should talk about the child in the third person. For example: "Hey, Dad, Kalani is feeling crummy right now. She's not feeling great about how this game ended, and I can sure understand that. It's not nice when you feel like people misunderstand you or they don't play by your rules."

Watch the child to see if they are okay with listening to what you are saying. If the child screams, "Shut up!" and covers their ears, you should say, "Oops, I'm hurting your ears; we can talk about this later." But if the child is okay with you talking to their parent, then you can continue: "Hey, I wonder if this is something that happens at home or at school a lot, too? If it does, that is a bad feeling—to constantly feel like people don't understand you or that life is super unfair. I wonder what that must be like? I wonder if I could guess?"

You might then ask the child to give you a thumbs up or a nod with their foot if it's okay for you to guess. If yes, you can try guessing: "I imagine it would feel very angering, like, *How come nobody is playing by my rules? How come people blame me for stuff when other people get away with things all the time?*"

If you get a signal from the child that you are on the right track, then provide validation. For more on the deliberate dialogue, refer back to chapters 3 and 8.

In fact, many apparent behavior problems within the play activities are natural launching-off points for entering into a deliberate dialogue about what is underneath the behavior. Because dyadic sessions are typically informed by parent updates, you often use these as the topic for your deliberate dialogue. However, you can use any number of the child's behaviors in the play section of the session to develop into a relational theme that you can then talk about, explore, and get more curious about.

I hope this chapter offers you a sense of possibility. Like any framework, IAFT can pose challenges to effective implementation. However, I created IAFT to support therapists as they help establish a sense of safety and connection for parents and children. When we focus on this goal—on *being with* children and on supporting parents as they learn to *be with* their children too—we see the magic of meaningful, regulated relationships.

Conclusion

Interrupting
Intergenerational Trauma

The magic of IAFT is not only in the support it offers to children; it is also in the support it offers to parents. The course of care can strengthen a child's attachment security, resiliency, and sense of self through play, parent work, and deliberate dialogue, and the parent's resiliency and sense of self is often strengthened too. In fact, although it is the therapist who offers guidance, the power of IAFT is frequently unlocked by the parent. When a parent is supported in offering their whole self to their child, and in learning to follow the therapist's lead in PACEful play and dialogue, they not only disrupt the dysregulation in their relationship with their child—they might also disrupt the legacy of dysregulation wrought by intergenerational trauma. To conclude this book, I'd like to tell the story of one such parent.

John began IAFT because he didn't know where else to turn for help in dealing with his son's behavioral challenges. At first, John was skeptical of and unwilling to engage in play, parent-only sessions, or PACEful interventions. However, with the support provided by IAFT, particularly in the parent-only sessions, he was able to gain new insight into his autobiographical narrative, which allowed him to develop a deeper and more nuanced sense of self. This insight not only strengthened John's own resiliency but also supported meaningful and enduring change through a deeper connection with his son.

John never meant to become a client, but when he brought his 11-year-old son, Adam, to see me, I insisted he come too. John was busy, and his entire identity was his family business: He owned a wood processing plant and a small horse farm, and he worked all the time, even on weekends. However, Adam's mom worked the swing shift as a nurse and could not be available for after-school IAFT sessions.

Adam had anxiety and executive functioning deficits and had been diagnosed with attention-deficit/hyperactivity disorder (ADHD) and oppositional defiant disorder. When I asked John about his experience parenting Adam, John said, "Adam is in his own world. He doesn't listen. Even simple things like clearing his cereal bowl from the table is something. I have to tell him three times. Same with most everything else. Doing his chores, going to school, going to bed—whatever we say, he stalls and doesn't listen." At the time I met Adam, he was on three different psychotropic medications, including a sedative for sleeping.

When I talked to Adam, he told me what he thought the problem was: "I can't think straight sometimes. I forget. Like when my dad tells me to do something, it sounds far away. Then he gets mad and yells at me."

"How does that feel to you?"

"Not good."

I then asked Adam about the anxiety and fears that the psychiatrist was medicating him for. He explained, "I can't sleep at night because I'm scared someone is going to crawl through the window. My dad tells me that's impossible because we're so high up, but my sister can climb the tree. And I hate taking the bus to school, because this older kid and his friends keep messing with me—they make fun of me and sometimes they tear up my notebooks and stuff. Also, I'm scared of Kiko, one of our mares, because she gets scared by critters, and twice she kicked me in the head when she saw a mouse."

"How do you deal with these fears?"

"I try to tell my dad that I don't want to muck the stalls. I'll fill the trough and the water buckets and stuff, but I don't want to go in behind her because she gets spooked so easily."

I turned to John and asked, "Is that a fair deal—Adam will take care of the chores outside of the stall but won't go in?"

John replied, "That's fine for now, but it's not really a solution. Adam has to learn that he's in charge. Horses are social animals. If you're scared, they're scared. But if you're confident, they are as calm as can be."

This, it turned out, was John's parenting philosophy. Whenever Adam was scared, John told him he had to put mind over matter and be courageous. This also applied to Adam's fears about going to sleep alone at night and the bully Adam was dealing with on the school bus.

John was resistant to play in the dyadic sessions, so I tried several different tactics to help him understand that this philosophy wasn't working for his son. I led deliberate dialogues to help Adam express how he felt unprotected and judged for his fears. I educated John in parent-only sessions about the brain and how admonitions and lectures can't help a frightened child. I recommended John do chores with his son, integrating a sense playfulness in the activities, instead of ordering Adam to do his chores by himself.

John always nodded in seeming accordance. However, the next week, Adam would report that things around the house were the same. John would ask Adam to go to bed but wouldn't tuck him in; John would tell Adam to muck the stalls alone even though we agreed they'd do it together; John would yell at Adam for dawdling before school even though he knew about Adam's fear of the bullies on the bus. When I asked John why he couldn't implement our strategies, he said he was tired at the end of the day and couldn't muster the energy to do Adam's chores with him. He also expressed in exasperation, "Adam is going to have to manage the factory when he's older. If he can't stand up to a horse or a kid on the bus, how is he going to be the boss of 35 workers at the factory?"

When I asked John about his relationship with his father in parent-only sessions, he told me that he revered him. He described his father as a hardworking war hero devoted to his community. Rather than a personal account, John's description of his father sounded like a reporter's account of a man on a far-off pedestal. When I asked for specific adjectives to describe his relationship with his father, John offered the words *kind*, *strict*, and *inspiring*. I asked if he had specific memories for those adjectives. For *strict*, John described the work ethic his father imposed on him and his brothers, requiring them to help at the factory and around their large property as well as maintain excellent grades and play football in high school. For *inspiring*, he noted that his father helped rebuild the town's church with his own hands after a portion of it had burned down. For *kind*, John chuckled as he recalled that he once disobeyed curfew and when he came in the front door, his dad was sitting in the dark with a rifle across his lap. John laughed and said he jumped five feet in the air, he was so scared, but his dad didn't say a word and didn't punish him. "That was his way of showing mercy on me."

Noticing a dismissive pattern of attachment, I pointed out that John's father seemed quite frightening, as with the example of the gun. John went on a long explanation defending his father and the wisdom of his ways. He kept repeating that he was much softer than John's grandfather, a volatile, angry man who beat John's father. "He was a tough SOB," he told me. "He came to the US as a poor immigrant at 19 with nothing but his work ethic. My grandfather provided for his family and he's the reason why I was able to go to college."

"Wow," I said, "Your grandpa had some really admirable qualities, but I saw you shudder as you spoke about him. What do you think made you shudder just then?"

"He died when I was six, but the stories my dad told—he was *not* someone you wanted to cross."

I pointed out that dealing harshly with boys seemed to be a repeated pattern in their family.

"Well, you had to back then!" John said defensively. "I don't think you understand the generation of men who came here and built their lives from scratch." As he said it, he smirked with derision. I noticed it made me feel small and naive, and I realized that must be how Adam felt when his dad lectured him.

"John, you seem to think I'm saying your grandfather or father was bad or that I don't appreciate their struggles. I think it's admirable you're defending them, but you seem worried about my pointing out that they were scary men at times. I wonder why that's so hard for you to talk about?"

"Because you don't understand!" John said. "They had to do what they did to me in order to get me to where I am!"

"What did they do to you?"

"My dad did scare the shit out of me at times. Once, he locked me in the tool shed for a whole evening because I'd gotten in trouble at school for punching another kid's science fair display. We'd both done a project on solar eclipses, except his diorama had electricity wired in and looked really good. I'd worked so hard on mine without any help. When I saw this kid's project, and what his dad had helped him do, I just flipped my lid.

"The teacher called my parents, and I knew I was in trouble. I ran home and hid under the bed until my dad came home and put me in the tool shed. It was so hot in there I thought I was going to die. He brought me water once in a while, but then just closed and bolted the door. When he finally let me out, the only thing he said was, 'You're not going to get anywhere by being jealous. If you want to be the best, you have to try harder.'"

As John talked about his experience, I could see he had flashes of fear, anger, and sadness, and I made a point of using my SES to demonstrate an intense focus and presence, nodding my head and expressing empathy in my voice. I asked John, "Do you think it's possible to respect your father and understand why he felt he needed to do that to you, while at the same time honoring the fact that, as a young boy, you were scared by what he did to you?"

"I don't know," John responded in a faraway voice.

"I want you to consider that you were a boy who had his own thoughts and wishes, his own feelings, who wanted to be accepted and recognized."

Again, John got a faraway look, as if contemplating this idea, and then he seemed to come to. He looked at me and said, "What does this have to do with Adam's problems?"

"I think Adam feels he can't have fears or ask for your help without you scaring him and making him feel bad for those feelings, just like your father did to you and your grandfather did to your father," I explained. "I don't think Adam has anxiety or ADHD. I think that he senses from you that it's not okay to feel scared or unsure. So, when he feels that way, he has to hide those feelings, but guess what? Those feelings don't go away. They get pushed down and then come out as having irrational fears and not being able to concentrate."

"Well, I was raised that way and I turned out okay!" John barked.

"At what cost?" I asked.

He paused. "What cost? I'm happy the way I am. I don't have any problems."

"Well, maybe that's true, but do you ever feel lonely or empty? Do you ever isolate from your wife even though she wants to be with you? Do you yell at Adam for not wanting to fall asleep alone even though we'd agreed in here that you'd sit with him until he falls asleep?"

John then told me he spent every night in his garage playing video games and gambling online. He hadn't lost any money, he assured me, but his wife was furious at him for staying in there and ignoring her feelings.

"John," I said, "You have to decide whether you're satisfied with the way you're functioning in your family right now. I can't decide that."

John tried one more time to defend himself. "But how is sitting in Adam's room until he falls asleep going to teach him independence and courage?! He's almost 12, and he needs me to read him a story and hold his hand on the bus? If he can't get his act together, he'll run the factory to the ground when he's older!"

"I want the same thing for Adam as you do. I want him to have a clear, healthy mind and be able to hold down a good job and function in society. But here's the thing—forcing Adam to do things he's afraid of is impeding his ability to gain the independence you're striving to teach him. By forcing him to muck Kiko's stall even though he's already been kicked in the head by her doesn't respect his experience of fear. Just like your father misunderstood and humiliated you for being jealous of your classmate's project.

"Your dad didn't ask you what it was that made you feel so bad that day when you saw your classmate's project. Instead, he made you feel really ashamed, lonely, and scared. Imagine if he'd asked you about what it was like for you to feel so proud and then so crestfallen when your classmate had such a superior science project."

John got quiet.

"What do you think it would've been like?" I asked.

John choked back tears as he mumbled, "That boy's father was at the science fair helping him rig up the electricity, and they looked so happy together. My dad would never have had the time, or even thought to help me."

"That makes so much sense, John. You wanted your dad to be with you, to enjoy you. And seeing your classmate get that was too painful, so you got angry and violent instead. And then you got scared of what your dad would do. You were taught to hide when you had feelings that were 'weak.' But actually, being able to be with someone who loves you when you have those feelings is what makes you feel stronger."

This was the beginning of productive therapy with John. It took us about five months of weekly sessions for him to see the impact of his own experiences as a child, and how the legacy of violence, loss, and fear played into his parenting attitudes toward Adam.

One of the most important things John and I worked on was honoring the fact that his father had done the best he could, while also acknowledging that, as a child, John had real and legitimate emotional needs and wishes. We then worked on expressing empathy for John's young self as he endured isolating and invalidating experiences with his father. During this process, John remembered several other disturbing and frightening incidents where his father intimidated and humiliated him in his efforts to raise him up to be "a strong man." John learned to express self-compassion for himself for these experiences.

Once John had come to terms with his childhood trauma, we turned our attention to his ability to repair his connection with Adam. John had to take responsibility for invalidating and scaring Adam, compromising Adam's sense of safety. In one touching session, John was able to look his son in the eye and fully engage in deliberate dialogue, apologizing for forcing Adam to muck the stall even though Kiko had twice kicked him in the head and saying how sorry he was for making Adam feel like his fears were not valid.

John was also able to communicate to Adam that it was hard for him to allow Adam to express his fear because John was taught that being sad or afraid was wrong. John told Adam that he was learning to approach things differently than his own father did. Adam began to ask about his grandfather, and John shared the good but also the uncomfortable and frightening aspects of the way he was raised. He talked about Adam's great-grandfather, and later, he and Adam looked up information together on Finland, where his great-grandfather was from.

In a subsequent dyadic session, the three of us discussed how scary events can be passed down from one generation to another. Adam, who was an amazing artist, helped to represent a different kind of passage, drawing a series of pictures of his great-grandfather leaving his seven siblings, crossing the ocean, and working in a lumber yard before buying their family farm. I encouraged Adam and John to discuss how this ancestor might have felt, not to justify his brutal behavior, but to have compassion for his legacy of tragedy and fear. This is an important aspect of healing—the inherited history can be named, honored, and then ceremoniously set aside as an artifact rather than as an active element to be passed down from generation to generation.

The final piece of the therapy in healing the attachment security between father and son was teaching John about the importance of joyful play, physical proximity, and touch. The play in the dyadic sessions, which John had initially been so resistant to, helped to foster attachment security and lay the groundwork for a healthier, whole sense of self. John had had no experience of affection, tenderness, or nurturing in his childhood. Therefore, he had no idea how to be present for another person on a physical level.

As the dyadic sessions strengthened John and Adam's connection through play and SES elements, especially touch, John became more open to staying close to his son during bedtime, including sitting shoulder to shoulder and stroking Adam's hair. He also started to see the importance of storytelling as a way to calm Adam's anxious brain. It turned out that, when given the freedom to be by Adam's side, John enjoyed lying next to Adam and making up adventure stories. Adam's nighttime problems eased.

As for the school fears, John tried to advocate for a bus monitor to prevent bullying, but that didn't work. He next tried meeting Adam at the bus stop to give the bully an intimidating look, but that only made things worse. Then one session, when they came in and I asked how the week went, Adam said, "It was great. Dad drove me to school every day." My eyes widened in surprise, and I looked at John.

"Yeah," he shrugged. "I don't want Adam to waste his energy having to worry about some twerp on the bus. I figure let him start out his day without that hassle so he can focus on learning."

Adam nodded. It was a much better week.

In the end, even the powerful intergenerational legacy of trauma within a family can be transformed once its relevance to a current problem is identified and the family members become motivated to see their struggles in a new light. The key to change in this case was creating a new narrative that superseded the old patriarchal legacy and opened the way for John and Adam to connect in ways that created a new, more fulfilling narrative for their relationship. Their newly playful, physically close, in-sync interactions demonstrated that the past, no matter how entrenched, is not destiny and need not determine the future. It may not be magic, but the change brought about by IAFT can be absolutely magical for families.

Appendix A

Speaking for the Child in Session

Typically, the IAFT therapist speaks for the child during a deliberate dialogue. The main goal of this work is to guide and deepen the connection between the child and parent.

Steps for Speaking for the Child

1. Determine the deeper emotion for the child, guessing if necessary.

2. Set the scene:

    a. Ask the child's permission to share with the parent: "Can we tell your mom (or dad, etc.) about this?"

    b. Ask the child if they prefer to speak for themselves or if they want you to talk for them.

3. If the child indicates they would like you to speak for them, let the child and parent know that you will be speaking for the child: "Okay, I'll talk for you as if I'm you. If I say something wrong, let me know."

    a. If the child looks nervous (or is hiding behind a pillow), explain: "You can also give a thumbs up, thumbs down, or thumbs sideways to tell me if I'm on the right track."

    b. Before beginning to talk for the child, take a deep breath, move a little in your body, and get a little closer to the child. This marks the transition to persona-taking with an obvious shift.

4. Begin with the following phrase: "Mom (or Dad, etc.), sometimes I feel like . . ."

    a. It is important to qualify the expression with "sometimes," as opposed to implying "always," in order to build in flexibility and the possibility for change.

5. Leave space for the parent to respond.

6. If the parent responds with a PACEful attitude—acceptance and empathy, in particular—continue the dialogue.

7. If the parent needs help expressing a PACEful attitude, prompt or guide them to respond with empathy and acceptance, or give them the words they need.

8. Continue giving the parent guidance until the child sees that the parent is able to soften and open up.

9. Zoom out for the parent and reflect what you have seen: "You did something very courageous by talking in this honest and open way."

10. Keep in mind that when speaking for the child, it is important to focus on the deeper feelings, such as loneliness, self-doubt, and fear. Do not emphasize anger for too long. Anger is the surface feeling. There are always more vulnerable feelings underneath. If anger is the object of focus, the parent will likely struggle to empathize.

Common Challenges to Speaking for the Child

What should you do if a parent tries to reassure the child as you are speaking for the child? Consider the following example, in which the therapist is talking for the child about the child's experience that they don't want to do homework because they feel that they are stupid.

> THERAPIST [*speaking as the child*]: Mom, sometimes when I have to do homework, I get so confused. I just feel like I'm stupid and I'll never be able to do it.

> MOM: No, you're not stupid. You are really smart!

Although the parent is trying to reassure the child, in fact they are denying rather than accepting their child's feelings. As a consequence, the parent cannot express empathy and cannot activate the PACEful response that would enable the parent to *be with* their child.

In this situation, you have two options:

1. Stay in the role of the child and say something like, "But, Mom, don't you understand? I feel like I am dumb and like I'll never be able to do the work."

2. Break out of the role-play to give the parent a direct suggestion of what to say, such as: "Mom, can you say something like, 'Wow, you

have a lot of doubts about yourself, and it's getting in the way of your being able to do your homework. I can understand why feeling that way would make it hard to complete your worksheet.'"

Because the goal is for the child to see and experience the parent allowing their feelings, understanding their feelings, and helping them see that those feelings make sense, it may be necessary to experiment with your options until the parent is able to express acceptance and empathy that the child can truly feel.

The PACE Attitude: A Guide for Parents

The PACE attitude is a way of interacting with your child, especially around difficult topics or situations, that will help them feel less defensive and more connected and understood. When you use the PACE attitude, you express *playfulness*, *acceptance*, *curiosity*, and *empathy*.

Playfulness

Playfulness does not mean persistent teasing or sarcasm. Playfulness means bringing in a lighthearted, joyful, energetic, and silly energy to your interactions with your child. It can sometimes mean winking or walking in a funny way, or making a silly sound when you are imitating something humorous, absurd, or ironic that you experience in day-to-day life. Playfulness has an upbeat, sometimes irreverent, sometimes self-deprecating tone that helps to dissipate tension and create moments of connection. Being playful or finding humor shows your child that life is not always serious, that you don't take yourself too seriously, and that you can find humor and pleasure in the little things in life.

While it's not appropriate to be playful when your child is feeling very upset, being humorous or playful when your child is mildly upset can divert their attention and steer them toward a lighter tone. It can surprise them and give them a reset. For instance, if your child is upset because they're hungry and want a sugary treat, you might respond in a silly, Cookie Monster voice: "Yummy yum yum—I've got the munchies too! Let's find something that will give us more energy to play!"

Acceptance

Acceptance means showing that you acknowledge and flow with what your child is saying, wishing, or feeling. You show acceptance by reacting without judgment, shock, or dismay at what they are expressing.

This attitude of acceptance does not mean condoning or accepting misbehavior or not providing limits. You can have strong limits and consequences and still accept the intention underneath your child's misbehavior.

For example, say you receive a call from school that your daughter hit another student when they got into an argument on the playground. When you ask your daughter to tell you about it, she says, "I hate that girl! She deserved to get hit because she knocked my block tower down on purpose." Responding with acceptance means saying something like "Wow, you felt really strongly about that" or "Thanks for telling me what was happening to you at the time." Your words in no way imply that it is okay to hit. It is simply a way to open a conversation about a difficult topic without shutting down your child and getting into an argument. Remember that there will be time later to clarify your expectations or to give a consequence.

Some other general acceptance statements could be:

- Thanks for telling me what's on your mind.

- I could tell that was important for you to express.

- I get it.

- I hear you.

- I got you.

- I can understand what you are saying.

- I didn't know you felt that way before.

- I understand that you don't need my help with this.

- I hear you saying you don't want to talk about this.

- I have definitely seen you being able to handle this on your own.

- From hearing your story, I can see why you feel that way.

Empathy

Empathy means making your child feel like you truly get it, like you can feel their underlying feelings and see things from their point of view. This is demonstrated not only through your words but also through your facial expressions, tone of voice, and body posture. By showing your child that you are willing to put yourself in their shoes, you allow them to feel that they are not alone with their distress. Even if their feelings are big and overwhelming, you are showing that their feelings are not too much for you to handle.

Showing empathy can be difficult to do, especially if your child is expressing anger and disappointment toward you. However, in these circumstances, it's even more important to try to convey empathy for your child's experience. Continuing our example of your daughter hitting her classmate and then telling you, "I hate that girl! She deserved to get hit because she knocked my block tower down on purpose," an empathic statement to this might be "Wow, that must have been so frustrating for you! You worked hard on the tower, and then your classmate knocked it down. And it felt like she did it on purpose!"

Here are some other general examples of empathy:

- That must be hard.
- I would be sad/mad/disappointed, too, if that happened to me.
- You've had to do this on your own for so long.
- Wow, so you have been dealing with a lot of difficult things.
- It must be really tough for you to handle all of this on your own.
- It must be hard for you to talk about this with me.
- Telling your story is never easy.
- You must be working really hard to cope on your own.

You can also express empathy through tones and sounds like *ooh, wow, jeez, ah,* and *uh-huh.*

Curiosity

Expressing curiosity with your child means asking questions that demonstrate that you truly wish to understand what is on their mind, how they see the world, and what their perspective is. It is not an interrogation or a quiz on how they could have handled the situation differently. It is a wondering aloud of what it would be like to be them in this situation.

True curiosity is demonstrated most strongly by your tone of voice. For the previous situation, an example of a true curiosity question would be "I wonder what made you so very upset that you lashed out at your classmate?" This is said in a wondering tone, with an upward inflection at the end of the question to demonstrate true interest. Contrast that with the tone of "Why did you do that?!" The latter typically sounds accusatory, demanding, and angry. The difference between curiosity and accusation is often in the way you say it. If your voice is not relaxed, or if your face and body are tense, then your child will feel the judgment, even if you use the so-called right words.

By being truly curious, you will help your child reflect on what they feel inside—what they think, believe, wish, and want. This is so valuable because when a child is aware of their thoughts and motives, it helps them feel like they know who they are on the inside. This knowledge guides them toward making decisions in the future that are in harmony with their goals and identity.

Other examples of curiosity include:

- Have you felt that way for a long time?

- What is it like?

- If there were one thing you would want me to understand about this situation, what would it be?

- Have you been in this situation before?

- Did anything ever help you to make things better about this problem?

- What could I do to help you get through this?

- What do you think the other person in this situation (your child's classmate, teacher, friend, sibling, etc.) believes is the problem?

- I wonder if you feel angry and unheard by being made to come to therapy?

- Do you have any ideas about why we're here in therapy together?

After you express a PACEful attitude, it is important to avoid giving long lectures or advice. It's also important to avoid sliding into an argument. Listen and consider what your child has said. If you need to make a decision on how to handle the situation or give a consequence, it's best to state it matter-of-factly.

Appendix C

VMA Games:
Activity Cards for Parents

2. Lights Out

The adult turns off the room's light, sits back down, and stays silent for one minute. The adult then turns the light back on.

4. Funny Faces

First, the adult makes a funny or silly face at their child and asks their child to copy it.

Next, the adult and child switch roles: The child makes a face and the adult copies it.

1. Balloon Toss

The adult and child toss the balloon back and forth, counting how many times they can pass the balloon while keeping it from dropping on the floor.

3. Story Time

The adult tells the child about a memory from the child's past.

Autonomic Timeline Template

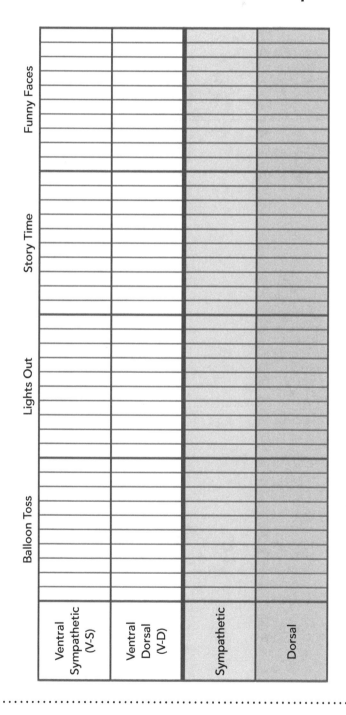

References

For your convenience, purchasers can download and print the
worksheets from this book from **www.pesipubs.com/dafna.lender**

Axline, V. M. (1969). *Play therapy*. Ballantine Books.

Booth, P. B., & Jernberg, A. M. (2010). *Theraplay: Helping parents and children build better relationships through attachment-based play* (3rd ed.). Jossey-Bass.

Bowlby, J. (1983). *Attachment: Attachment and loss* (2nd ed., Vol. 1). Basic Books.

Dana, D. A. (2018). *The polyvagal theory in therapy: Engaging the rhythm of regulation*. W. W. Norton.

Dana, D. A. (2020a). *Polyvagal exercises for safety and connection: 50 client-centered practices*. W. W. Norton.

Dana, D. A. (2020b). *Polyvagal flip chart: Understanding the science of safety*. Norton Professional Books.

Dana, D. A., & Porges, S. W. (2018). *Clinical applications of the polyvagal theory: The emergence of polyvagal-informed therapies*. W. W. Norton.

George, C., Main, M., & Kaplan, N. (1985). *Adult attachment interview (AAI)* [Database record]. APA PsycTests. https://doi.org/10.1037/t02879-000

Hughes, D. A. (2009, February 20). *Developing attachment: Family therapy examples, part 3: Parents* [Film; educational DVD]. Kinship Center.

Lieberman, A. F., & Van Horn, P. (2011). *Psychotherapy with infants and young children: Repairing the effects of trauma on early attachment*. Guilford Press.

Norris, V., & Lender, D. (2020). *Theraplay: The practitioner's guide*. Jessica Kingsley Publishers.

Perry, B. D., & Dobson, C. L. (2013). The neurosequential model of therapeutics. In J. D. Ford & C. A. Courtois (Eds.), *Treating complex traumatic stress disorders in children and adolescents: Scientific foundations and therapeutic models* (pp. 249–260). Guilford Press.

PESI. (2022). *EMDR: List of positive and negative cognitions*. https://www.pesi.com/blog/details/2098/emdr-list-of-positive-and-negative-cognitions

Porges, S. W. (1995). Orienting in a defensive world: Mammalian modifications of our evolutionary heritage. A polyvagal theory. *Psychophysiology, 32*(4), 301–318. https://doi.org/10.1111/j.1469-8986.1995.tb01213.x

Porges, S. W. (2004). Neuroception: A subconscious system for detecting threat and safety. *Zero to Three, 24*(5), 19–24.

Porges, S. W. (2009). The polyvagal theory: New insights into adaptive reactions of the autonomic nervous system. *Cleveland Clinic Journal of Medicine, 76*(4 suppl. 2), S86–S90. https://doi.org/10.3949/ccjm.76.s2.17

Porges, S. W. (2015). Making the world safe for our children: Down-regulating defence and up-regulating social engagement to 'optimise' the human experience. *Children Australia, 40*(2), 114–123. https://doi.org/10.1017/cha.2015.12

Porges, S. W. (2018). Polyvagal theory: A primer. In D. Dana & S. W. Porges (Eds.), *Clinical applications of the polyvagal theory: The emergence of polyvagal-informed therapies* (pp. 50–72). W. W. Norton.

Shah, P. E., Fonagy, P., & Strathearn, L. (2010). Is attachment transmitted across generations? The plot thickens. *Clinical Child Psychology and Psychiatry, 15*(3), 329–345. https://doi.org/10.1177/1359104510365449

Siegel, D. J. (2020). *The developing mind: How relationships and the brain interact to shape who we are* (3rd ed.). Guilford Press.

Siegel, D. J., & Hartzell, M. (2003). *Parenting from the inside out: How a deeper self-understanding can help you raise children who thrive.* Jeremy P. Tarcher/Penguin.

Steele, H., & Steele, M. (Eds.). (2008). *Clinical applications of the adult attachment interview.* Guilford Press.

Stern, D. N. (2004). *The present moment in psychotherapy and everyday life.* W. W. Norton.

Stern, D. N. (2000). *The interpersonal world of the infant: A view from psychoanalysis and developmental psychology.* Basic Books.

Trevarthen, C., & Aitken, K. J. (2001). Infant intersubjectivity: Research, theory, and clinical applications. *The Journal of Child Psychology and Psychiatry, 42*(1), 3–48. https://doi.org/10.1017/S0021963001006552

van der Kolk, B. (2014). *The body keeps the score: Brain, mind, and body in the healing of trauma.* Viking.

Winnicott, D. W. (1968). Playing: Its theoretical status in the clinical situation. *International Journal of Psychoanalysis, 49*(4), 591–599.

Zanetti, C. A., Powell, B., Cooper, G., & Hoffman, K. (2011). The circle of security intervention: Using the therapeutic relationship to ameliorate attachment security in disorganized dyads. In J. Solomon & C. George (Eds.), *Disorganized attachment and caregiving* (pp. 318–342). Guilford Press.

About the Authors

 **Dafna Lender, LCSW,** is an international trainer and supervisor for practitioners who work with children and families. She is a certified trainer and supervisor/consultant in both Theraplay® and dyadic developmental psychotherapy (DDP). Dafna's expertise is drawn from 25 years of working with families with attachment in many settings: at-risk after-school programs, therapeutic foster care, in-home crisis stabilization, residential care, and private practice. Dafna's style, whether as a therapist or teacher, combines the lighthearted with the profound by bringing a playful, intense, and passionate presence to every encounter. Dafna is the coauthor of *Theraplay: The Practitioner's Guide* (2020). She teaches and supervises clinicians in 15 countries in 4 languages: English, Hebrew, French, and Spanish.

Molly Gage, PhD, is a book developer and developmental editor who specializes in transformative nonfiction.